CROSS-COUNTRY SKIING FOR THE FUN OF IT

CROSS-COUNTRY

Illustrated with photographs and drawings

DODD, MEAD & COMPANY · NEW YORK

SKIING FOR THE FUN OF IT

Margaret Bennett

Second Printing

ISBN: 0-396-06860-X
Library of Congress Catalog Card Number: 73-9269
Printed in the United States of America
by Vail-Ballou Press, Inc., Binghamton, N. Y.

For Martin P. Dowling, the Irish *Langläufer*,
who first taught us to skinny ski

ACKNOWLEDGMENTS

FOR THIS BOOK there are more than the usual number of without-whoms-there-wouldn't-have-beens. There were our outstandingly excellent ski instructors, in order of their appearance: Ned Gillette, Hans Wiik, Trine Bech, Mead Hargis, and Wayne Merry. The few instructors who gave us the priceless gift of a bad example shall remain nameless.

There was A. Muller of Inter-Montana Sport, who helped ski touring by inventing the mohair-strip-bottomed ski and coining the "*Langläufer Leben Länger*" (Cross-country skiers live longer) motto, and who helped us by showering us with reams of reference material from his vast files. There was H. Juon, Assistant Director of the Swiss National Tourist Office in San Francisco, deliverer of the goods, both photographic and typographic, on the subject of Swiss ski touring.

There were Jeanne Parry of SAS and Poul Christiansen and Per Holte of the Los Angeles Scandinavian Tourist Office, who got our skis on the right tracks in Norway.

There were Roland Boire, Deputy Director of the Canadian Government Travel Bureau, and C. A. Watt, Manager of the Los Angeles office, who on one week's notice planned a clockwork excursion to Eastern Canada. There was Georges Girard, president of the Mont-Sainte-Anne Ski Club, who was our gallant Gallic guide to the touring in that environ of Quebec City. There was Dan Lewis, who found us wandering the Laurentian wilderness, took us home, provided us with photos and did us the honor of introducing us to Jack Rabbit Johannsen. And there was the Great Man himself, who gave us his inspiration —and his ski wax.

There were Betty Lucas and Birthe Wiik and Johannes von Trapp, who provided aid and comfort beyond the call of the innkeeper's duty.

There was Brad Haskell, president of Great World, who let us crib his best charts. There was Ralph Thornton, double threat man of the *Minneapolis Star,* who supplied us with words and photos and who looks great in a touring suit. There was Ben Rinaldo, publisher of *Skier,* who poured forth pungent quotes.

And most especially there was Marc Hardy, Director of the Tourist Information Division of the Government of Quebec, who is as talented a photographer as he is an enthusiastic a ski tourer and who was supremely generous with his talent, his time, and his Citroen.

Finally, there was that anonymous Norwegian of 4500 years ago who first whittled out skis. And there was—and still is—God, who makes the snow, albeit somewhat capriciously.

We praise them all.

BARBARA TOOHEY and JUNE BIERMANN
alias "MARGARET BENNETT"

CONTENTS

CROSS-COUNTRY SKIING
FOR THE FUN OF IT

1. GETTING TO KNOW IT

CROSS-COUNTRY skiing for the *fun* of it? Why else would you do it? asks the logical mouth attached to the logical mind. Well, think back to the televised winter Olympic games in Sapporo, Japan. Remember some of the cross-country racers making that last lung-bursting effort across the finish line, blood pouring from their noses? There may be triumph in that and the adrenalin kick of competition, but fun?

Then consider the annual fifty-three-mile Swedish Vasaloppet race, about which one American participant said, "I can't describe it. I thought I was going to die. My groin muscles were on fire." The men who take part in this racc have the solid satisfaction of meeting a grueling challenge to their powers of endurance and determination. But do they enjoy it?

And, finally, imagine the high-country tourer picking his way across avalanche territory, realizing that his next step may knock loose a lethal slab slide. Think of the fifty-pound pack on his back. Hear him gasp in the thin air. See the ice crystals forming in his hair and eyebrows and beard. And imagine how it's going to be at night when he digs out his snow cave and curls up to try to sleep with his stomach sloshing around the reconstituted freeze-dried chicken à la king, as a blizzard screeches overhead. This is *fun?*

Unless you are a card-carrying masochist or a compulsive daredevil, none of these cross-country activities could be called fun, at least not by Mr. Webster's definition of fun: "that which provides mirth and amusement" and for which he lists as synonyms "merriment, pleasure, play, gaiety, and frolic."

The fun of cross-country skiing is what this book is all about—the day, halfday, or even one- or two-hour tour through beautiful surroundings, the skill-honing at your own pace on a flat track, the leisurely skimming along marked and prepared trails, the cutting of your own route through the froth of fresh-fallen snow, the picnicking, the picture-taking, the companionship, the solitude, all the many and varied personal and universal joy-producing qualities of cross-country. Not the least of these joys is the return to home or to the lodge, where waits a hot bath for the restoration of your pleasantly weary body, a hot glühwein, a hot dinner, and if not a hot, at least a warm bed.

And just as we'll court the fun, we'll shun its opposite:

misery and its synonyms—tribulation, trial, suffering, grief, anguish, woe, and distress.

THE GAME OF THE NAME: The only really difficult thing about cross-country skiing is figuring out what to call it. Many purists consider cross-country (or X-C for short) to be the term used only for racing, while touring means anything else that you do on the skinny skis, except jumping. Others consider touring to mean that you have a heavy pack on your back and you're high up somewhere, like along the Continental Divide, slogging and shussing with fatter, heavier touring skis and cable bindings and practicing all those day and night survival skills. What these people would call the kind of relaxed touring I enjoy, I don't know. Maybe they don't even recognize its existence.

The United States Ski Association after a lengthy session of mouth-wrestling the nomenclature problem played it both ways by deciding to call its cross-country division "Ski Touring and Mountaineering."

The Silva Company, distributors of ski equipment, have come up with the term "Ski-Jogging," which they're so fond of they've registered it. Their Ski-Jogging® is "the enjoyable wintertime sport of touring on skis up and down hills, through beautiful woodlands, the flat countryside, around your yard, or even down a quiet back road."

To add to the verbal intricacies, we also have the generic term Nordic, which is often used to cover everything—X-C racing, touring, jumping, and even the glidey-glidey, bang-bang of the biathalon; everything, that is, except downhill, lift-served Alpine skiing.

Here and now, though, I'm going to follow the policy of Humpty Dumpty in *Through the Looking-Glass,* "When *I* use a word, it means just what I choose it to mean—neither more nor less." And I choose cross-country, X-C, ski touring, and Nordic to mean the same thing—that is to say, all that good stuff we do on skinny skis for fun.

Racing on X-C skis I shall call right out "cross-country ski racing." That survival bit in the high mountain wilderness I shall call "ski mountaineering" with the emphasis on the second word, because that's where I think it belongs.

I shall use Alpine and downhill interchangeably to refer to what Jean-Claude Killy does—on the slopes, that is.

SOMETHING OLD, SOMETHING NEW, SOMETHING BORROWED: Cross-country is old, as old as the 4,500-year-old Hoting ski discovered in Sweden and as old as the 4,000-year-old rock carving of a skier found on the island of Rødøy in Norway.

Cross-country is also new. It's as new as the ecology movement with which it has much in common. Take the United States Ski Association Ski Tourer's pledge:

"I will protect the land and the natural resources of the land on which I ski. I will make it my personal business to leave the land in such a condition that except for the tracks of my skis upon the snow, no one will ever know that I was there. I will always treat the land gently so that I may return in the future and be welcomed as an old friend."

And cross-country skiing is borrowed from the Scandinavian countries, where it all began as a wintertime necessity. As with fishing and sailing, over the years a life-giving necessity became a life-enhancing sport. Like borrowers of other valuable commodities, such as books and tools, we who have borrowed this sport become so attached to it that we have no intention of ever giving it back.

SKIING FOR PEOPLE WHO DON'T LIKE SKIING

Maybe you're a downhill dropout. Or maybe you never even dropped in on downhill for one or more of the many valid reasons you might have had for avoiding it. Strangely enough, the very reasons why you don't like downhill could well be the reasons why you will love cross-country.

THE BEST OF ALL POSSIBLE WORLDS: One of my friends who in her late forties took up cross-country after an on-again, off-again affair with downhill was ecstatic over the switch. "What I like most about cross-country," she said, "is it's so *possible.* When I used to watch those hot-shot downhill instructors flip a turn with everything up to and including their jaw muscles in perfect form, I knew that for me it was no use. I could never ski like that. I felt I was just wasting my time and money and battering my body and ego for nothing. But I can do cross-country, really *do it,* maybe not as fast as the pros, but almost as well and it makes me feel good all over."

Anyone can really *do it* just as long as he's ambulatory. That rusty old saw that grates on my mind every time I hear it, "If you can walk, you can ski," never was true about downhill and is too conservative for X-C. What it should be is, "If you can *shuffle,* you can cross-country."

In a German book on the sport they say, "*Skilanglauf für alle von acht bis achtzig*" (Cross-country skiing for everyone from eight to eighty). That's another understatement. Consider Jack Rabbit Johannsen, the ninety-seven-year-old living legend of the Laurentians. He's still going strong on his cross-country skis, stronger than those half or even a third his age. What with Jack Rabbit and the number of more than somewhat pregnant women I've seen on ski tours, perhaps the more appropriate motto for X-C would be the one the insurance companies use to describe the extent of their coverage: "From womb to tomb."

EVERY BODY NEEDS CROSS-COUNTRY SKIING: In Switzerland they have a motto, "*Langläufer Leben Länger.*" Translation: "Cross-country skiers live longer." I've been trying to come up with an equally catchy motto in English (Cross-country counteracts cardiacs? Cross-country conditions corpuscles? Cross-country creates centenarians?), but so far, obviously, I've failed, although all my mottoes, if not catchy, are true.

Cross-country skiing is the ideal exercise. Dr. Marvin Clein, head of the sports medicine team at the University of Denver, who tested athletes in all sports for physical condition, came to the conclusion that the cross-country skier is the most perfectly tuned of human machines. Everything gets a workout in X-C. As Lisa Dobloug, a former Norwegian ski pro and currently active in the health spa field, states, "Cross-country is super exercise for legs, the most complete I can think of, as well as for abdomen, midriff, arms, back, and shoulders. You are always outside, breathing fresh air. And it does as much for your mind as for your body."

It's aerobic; it's stretching; it's reducing. Depending on how fast you do it, it burns more calories than any other sports activity. Not that downhill skiing is not exercise and plenty of it. It's just that in Alpine the conditioning does not always involve the total body and it tends to come in spurts interspersed with lift-line standing and lift riding.

NOTHING BROKEN, NOTHING MAIMED: I have heard from some fanatic devotees of cross-country skiing that no one in the 4,500-year history of the sport has so much as broken a fingernail. This is, of course, ridiculous. You *can* get injured in X-C. A meteorite could, for example, strike you on the head or you could trip over a sluggish wolverine and bust your whatever. But, still, the danger *is* infinitely less than in downhill. Studies show that out of a hundred thousand downhill skiers fifty are likely to suffer a break or bad sprain, while out of a hundred thousand tourers only one or two run that risk. For example, it was not until the third year of operation of the X-C program at Yosemite that anyone was injured and this was a broken wrist caused by a fall on an ice patch.

As U. S. Ski Team coach John Caldwell says, "Bone breaks are still very rare." Cross-country, according to the Bratlie wax people, "is a safe sport for those who have to go to work on Monday mornings."

Cross-country white sale: In terms of equipment X-C is a bargain sport. Consider the cost figures of a quality outfit in both downhill and X-C:

	DOWNHILL	X-C
Skis	$110–$235	$25–$85
Poles	$15–$35	$6–$10
Bindings	$30–$65	$5–$8
Boots	$65–$170	$20–$40

This is just the beginning. Prices in Alpine equipment rise as high as the Jungfrau and, besides, downhill skiers in their endless search for the perfect schuss, the perfect turn, keep scrapping their equipment and buying new in hopes that the latest boots or edges or bindings or pole basket will be the decisive factor. An expensive proposition. In cross-country you know the equipment doesn't make all that much difference and you tend to hold onto what you have until it wears out, an ecologically as well as financially valid attitude.

Then there's the lift ticket. At the moment of this writing $9–$10 is not an uncommon figure, and by the time you read it, it will probably be $11–$12. A week's downhill vacation, then, is at least a cool $64 more than cross-country. To add to that, the only place you can do downhill is at a mountain ski resort with the accompanying high cost of living. Cross-country can be done virtually anywhere where there's snow.

Ski lessons cost around $5 for a half day. In X-C, unless you're out to become a racer, about two lessons are all you really need, and you could get away without those if you had to. Downhill lessons are like a drug habit. You keep needing another fix to make you feel right about yourself—get rid of that stem, perfect that wedel. Year after year after year after year. Dollar after dollar after dollar after dollar.

We'll discuss the differences in clothing required for the two sports later, but in terms of cost it could be summed up as House of Dior compared to Goodwill Industries.

GROUP THERAPY: Downhill skiing is always advertised as a great togetherness sport. I can't imagine why. Aside from those brief encounters on lifts, just about the only time people come together in downhill is when they have a head-on collision. The family that skis Alpine together comes apart the moment they hit the slopes. Each member immediately races off to his particular level, which is almost never the same as that of another member. They usually can't even find each other for lunch in the cafeteria mob scene.

In touring, on the other hand, the groups who go out together stay together and stop and talk together and eat lunch together and share experiences together.

PSYCHED IN: X-C is not an ego trip like downhill, where you have to keep perfecting your jet turns on Hara-Kiri Hill so you'll have something to brag about in the after-ski hours. Cross-country is more of a superego trip. In case you've forgotten your Freud, the superego is the ethical side of your nature. It's that mental structure that acts as your conscience and has the formidable job of mediating between your ego drives and your social ideals. If you're a stronger skier in touring, instead of using your prowess to put down, you can use it to help out by carrying the heaviest pack or by being the trail breaker through fresh snow.

FEAR STRIKES OUT: Many are the mornings on a downhill ski trip to a new area that you awaken with an empty space in the pit of your stomach about big enough to hold Sun Valley. As soon as you become fully conscious, fear rushes in to fill the space. Mainly, it's the fear of the unknown. What are the lifts going to be like? How hard will it be to get off them? How do they mark their runs here? Is intermediate *really* intermediate, or do they just mark a random sample of expert runs intermediate so they'll have some variety on the trail map? Will I be able to find a good route down or will I wind up trembling at the brink of a cornice? And then there are the known and remembered fears of bindings that don't release when you fall or that *do* release for no reason in the middle of a turn. There is that ever-present fear of the hordes of out-of-control skiers programmed to bash you.

With X-C there's none of that. It's always a relaxed, yawning, stretching greeting of the day with the secure knowledge that you're not going to get onto anything you can't handle. And even if you do get onto something like an icy slope where your Lignostone edges refuse to bite, all you have to do is snap off your bindings and stroll down to an easier area. No sweat, no strain, no loss of dignity. Especially there's no loss of dignity, because there isn't some critic dangling overhead on a chairlift analyzing your technique or lack thereof.

THE ART OF THE MATTER: Everything about cross-country is aesthetically pleasing. The thin, graceful wooden skis are a joy to see and to touch, especially something like the Madshus Birkebeiner skis, which, with their unfinished pine-tar impregnated tops, acquire over the years a patina like old silver.

There's the smell of the wax and the pine trees and the sounds of silence along the trail: the squeaking of the skis in the powder, the soft whuff as a tree drops a branchworth of snow the morning after a storm and perhaps the gentle wheeze of your out-of-shape companions on the trail or your out-of-shape self.

But most of all, there's the beauty of nature—the dark-green trees against the white backdrop, the animal tracks punched into your path and the light striking the snow, setting up reverberations of sparkle that make it look as if

Zsa Zsa Gabor dropped her jewel box.

Need I contrast this with a weekend afternoon at a downhill resort with the loudspeakers throwing rock at your eardrums, your fellow humans shoving you in the lift line and stomping all over your shiny new fluorescent orange fiberglass skis, the ski mountain shaved of its foliage and stabbed with lift supports, the air laden with the scent of gasoline and hamburger grease . . . no, I guess I needn't.

SKIING FOR PEOPLE WHO LIKE SKIING TOO MUCH

Now that I've applied the brass knuckles to downhill skiing, I have a confession to make. Even with all its sometime faults, I still adore it. It's as the old torch songs say, you've done me wrong and I'm black and blue and all shook up, and I think I'm going out of my head, still I've got you under my skin, and I can't get you out of my heart.

If X-C is for people who don't like Alpine skiing, paradoxically it's also for those of us who like it too much—too much to wait until the lifts start running in the fall, too much to stop when the lifts stop running in the spring, too much to sit around the lodge when the visibility is zero, too much to spend all our time standing in lift lines on crowded weekends and holidays, and too much to quit skiing just because we've run out of lift ticket money.

A lot of skiers feel they have to be either a downhill freak or an X-C head. They think they have to ally themselves with one group or the other, loudly defending their kind of skiing and sneeringly putting down the other guy's kind. Not so. X-C and downhill are the most compatible of activities. This is one of the few times in life you can have it both ways. It's like a balanced power home with both the steady glowing gas of X-C and the flashing electricity of downhill. It's like red and white wine. You may prefer a hearty burgundy with one meal and yet on another occasion a cool, light Vourvray may be more to your taste. X-C is like love and downhill is like sex. You *can* have one without the other, but if you want to get the full double whammy out of life, you're crazy not to go for both.

SKI TO MAKE READY: If downhill *is* your big thing, cross-country can make it even bigger for you. Ski instructors report that for most people the first downhill trip of the season is just that—downhill all the way. They arrive at the resort in a high state of enthusiasm but a low state of physical readiness. It's usually one day of mad activity and three of recuperation. *But* if a skier has warmed up on the sparse snows of home with cross-country skiing, he is totally ready to squeeze the last drop of juice out of his downhill vacation.

And X-C can further enhance your Alpine pleasure all season long, if you alternate the two. X-C will give you the endurance you need for downhill, as well as providing muscle tone in the arms, legs, and feet.

DOUBLE YOUR PLEASURE, DOUBLE YOUR FUN: "If the weather is cold and bitter, you do better at *Langläuf* than skiing down a high mountain where the wind is sharp, but if you get a sunshine day it is better to ski downhill than through the woods." That's Paul Niff, ski school director in Pontresina, Switzerland, talking. He personally uses X-C for conditioning and downhill for sport and advocates both for his pupils if they want a well-rounded ski program.

Not only can X-C improve a ski vacation, it can literally save it. The skinny skis can function on the thinnest and lousiest of snow. If you find yourself on a ski vacation trying to negotiate rocks and dirt and ice, don't despair and defect to the bar or bail out for home. Just smear the klister on your touring skis and head for the woods and a separate-but-equal-in-terms-of-enjoyment experience.

Taking up cross-country adds another string to your winter sports banjo. You can make twice as much beautiful music.

2. EQUIPMENT

First, you go out and buy all your equipment. Yes, *buy* and, yes, *all*—skis, bindings, boots, poles. In downhill the advice is usually to rent equipment until you see if you really like the sport. With X-C there is little risk. At the very least, you'll like it. In all probability you'll love it. Witness the fact that many cross-country ski schools will refund you the cost of your first lesson if you don't enjoy it. I've never heard of a downhill ski school making that offer.

Another reason you should buy right off is that since X-C equipment is so relatively inexpensive, in just a few days' rental you pay enough to have bought the equipment in the first place. If, however, you are the super-cautious type who just can't bring yourself to buy before you try, there are some rental shops who will allow you to apply your first day's rental to the purchase price.

OLDIES BUT BADIES: One thing I beg you not to do is to take an old stiff, beat-up pair of downhill skis, attach a leftover set of cable bindings, don an old pair of hiking boots or broken-down Alpine ski boots and slog off. For slogging it would be. When you set off on the totally wrong equipment, you reduce your F.Q. (Fun Quotient) to a minus quantity.

You need the lightweight touring skis and boots and pin bindings to get all the kicks—and glides—the sport has to offer. If money is short, sell your firstborn to the Gypsies or set up your dear gray grandmother in an apple stand, but *do not use leftover Alpine equipment for ski touring.* Not that it isn't done, but like driving with your emergency brake on, it is not recommended.

IN THE MARKETPLACE: The big question is where to buy your X-C equipment. In general, I've found that the shops that celebrate their mountaineering departments are a better bet than the shops that place their major emphasis on downhill skiing. X-C and mountaineering have natural emotional ties, more, it seems, than downhill and X-C. The personnel in the mountaineering shops often have been into ski touring as their wintertime counterpart of summer hiking and backpacking and camping long before X-C became the popular sport that it is now. The downhill shop people sometimes have had only a crash course weekend clinic—if that—to make them come on with the right sounds while pushing the product. The worst part about these instant experts is that they don't have the hot-eyed enthusiasm of the True Believer in

X-C. You'll want to have a True Believer to help you with your selection, not just because he'll be more capable of helping you get what you need, but because he'll be willing to talk endlessly with you on the subject.

Any well-stocked X-C shop should have at least three kinds of skis to choose from—one of which should be the no-wax variety. It should also have more than one brand of boot and more than one style. Naturally, it should have a complete selection of one brand of wax, even better two or three, plus blow torches, scrapers, and everything else you need to do the wax thing. Another good indication of the caliber of the shop is whether it has the facilities to do the pine tarring of your bases for you; most new wooden skis require this protective treatment.

KEEP IT LIGHT: Although infinite subtle variations are starting to appear on the X-C equipment scene, in general there are three levels of equipment available for three distinct types of X-C: racing, touring, and light touring.

Racing equipment, as you might suspect from its name, is for racing. The skis are the narrowest and the lightest (48 mm or less in width and 3 pounds or under in weight). The boots are the thinnest and the most flexible. They are, in fact, almost like track shoes. The bindings are the rat trap pin style that leaves your heel free.

Racing equipment is only effective on a prepared track when used by the most pro, the most conditioned of *Langläufers.* The skis are likely to break on the kind of tour that those of us who are out for the fun of it do. The boots are likely to bone-chill feet that are not hotfooting it around a racing track. Do not buy racing equipment. At least, not now. If some strange ego drive compels you to get racing skis, at least get what's called "extra-light touring," which is a more durable version of the emaciated skinny skis.

Touring skis are the widest and the heaviest (56–60 mm wide and about 5½ pounds), and the boots are high-topped and sturdier. These wider skis used to be the most popular. Now, however, they are recommended only for those whose idea of touring is going off into the nowhere with a backpack or for those who have a really serious problem with balance and need a more solid platform, or for those who do most of their touring on dry powder and need a wider board to float on it. You also may need the broader-based touring skis if you are so large and heavy that your weight would punch the tails of the narrower skis into the snow.

Now we come to the happy medium—light touring equipment (skis 50–56 mm wide and weighing about 4½ pounds). This is what you want when you're doing X-C for the fun of it, sometimes on prepared tracks, sometimes on trails or snowbound roads, and sometimes in untracked open spaces or woods. The boots can be low-cut or over-the-ankle, although the low-cut variety is now more popular, because they're lighter. (I also suspect that it's because they're less Li'l Abner-looking.) The bindings you use for light touring are the same pin type the racers use.

Unlike many of life's middle grounds, light touring

equipment is not just a compromise. It has managed to take the best from racing equipment (good performance, light weight, and graceful appearance) and mate it with the best from touring equipment (durability and stability).

Waxing and waning: Within the general light touring category you still have a number of choices to make. These choices will be determined not so much by absolutes as by your own psychological and physiological makeup.

The first great decision you must make is whether to buy skis that require waxing or skis that don't. In order to decide whether you're going to be a wax lover (waxophile) or a wax hater (waxophobe), answer the following questions:

1. Do you prefer poker and crap shooting to chess and bridge; calling on the telephone to writing a letter; hiring someone to fill out your income tax form to doing it yourself?

2. Do you prefer a car with a stick shift to one with an automatic transmission?

3. Are you a good cook?

4. Do you almost always have more than average ability in any sport you take up?

5. How are you fixed for free time; are you pretty well boxed in by your job, family responsibilities, etc.?

Now let's analyze your answers.

1. If you're a poker-playing, crap-shooting telephone addict who can't stand putting down all those stupid numbers on that idiotic form, then you're probably the impatient type and hence a waxophobe.

It takes a lot of patience to bubble pine tar into your ski soles, put on perhaps a base wax, and then on each tour select the proper wax for the day's conditions. It takes even more patience if you discover you've waxed wrong and have to add another layer of softer wax. And it takes a whole slag heap of patience if it turns out you have to scrape or blow-torch off the softer wax and put on a harder one.

2. If you drive a car with a stick shift—especially a 4-on-the-floor—you're probably a waxophile. You don't mind putting forth effort if it means you get closer to perfection in your driving or your skiing. If little nuances of speed and handling and feel of the road are important to you, little nuances of speed and handling and feel of the snow will be important to you as well. No doubt you wouldn't think of doing anything but waxing.

3. If you're a good cook, you're used to following recipes and, even more important, you're used to playing it by instinct and making on-the-spot variations. You're also used to mucking around with pots of viscous substances. All of these abilities are important in cross-country ski waxing, and if you have them you have a head start toward being a waxophile.

4. If you're the athletic type, you should be a waxophile. Only with waxing can you get the maximum performance out of your skis—the longest glide and the

greatest speed. You'll want the maximum performance out of your skis to keep up with the maximum performance you usually get out of your body.

If you're not particularly athletic—a kind of Sunday afternoon stroller on skis—you probably will never develop enough technique to notice much difference between a well-waxed ski and the kind that requires no waxing; so don't make trouble for yourself.

5. If you're strapped for time, even if you're by nature a waxophile, you may be by necessity a waxophobe. Waxing, like art, is long. It takes a long time of doing it to learn what you're doing. When you don't have much time, you'll probably want to spend it actually skiing and not getting ready to ski or cleaning up after skiing.

Most of us emerge from this test as waxoschizos, but try to drop yourself into one slot or the other and proceed.

SKIS FOR WAXOPHOBES

Fur and Fishscales sounds like the title of a new magazine for outdoorsmen, but in reality it is a description of the two kinds of waxless bases you can have on cross-country skis.

FUR PIECE: The furred bottoms are based on the old idea of climbing skins. The skins were slipped over the skis so that when you walked uphill the fur was rubbed the wrong way and you hung on and didn't slip backwards. When you got to the top, you took off the climbing skins and slid down.

The modern X-C variation of climbing skins has two parallel mohair strips running lengthwise down the kicking area (the center one-third of the ski). These strips enable you to trot uphill and then since they're being rubbed the right way on the downhill, they let you slide with a little help from the plastic bases.

Many X-C-ers swear by these. They're particularly popular in the Alps, and they're catching on here. In fact, one big X-C rental shop in a major Colorado resort rents nothing else but these and uses them in all their lessons. I must admit, though, I developed a certain amount of suspicion about this shop's true motivation when one of the attendants said, "Yeah, we like these a lot better. Last year when we were using the regular skis, we ended up waxing forty pairs of skis every morning. What a drag!"

Objections to the mohair strips include the fact that they wear out and have to be replaced periodically. In terms of performance, the main drawback is that they just don't glide as well as well-waxed skis. I've heard it is said by fanatic waxophiles that you can lose up to 80 percent of your glide. A definite disadvantage is the way mohair freezes up when it gets wet and this eliminates both climbing and gliding power. The manufacturer, however, has worked out a better waterproofing system so the latest models will be more frost-free.

The story of the fur bottoms is well summed up by the catalogue of one of the largest snow sporting goods companies (and you can believe what they say since they stock a great number of skis that require waxing): ". . . this is the first waxless ski we have yet seen that performs well under a wide range of snow conditions. Although an excellent wax job can hardly be surpassed, [the mohair strip type ski] provides a very acceptable alternate."

SCALING THE MOUNTAIN: Another recent no-wax innovation is the layered plastic bottom that has a rearward sloping pattern that resembles fish scales. These skis grab during the kick and the climb, yet slide during the glide and descent. To a certain extent. They share with the mohairs the glide loss inherent in any nonwaxed ski. I've also heard of water getting in under the fish scales and freezing and playing havoc with the lamination and camber. But this is more of a rare occurrence than a regular happening. There have been complaints, too, that they wear out, but then so do wooden skis and people and everything else in the world. Another whine is that they make a funny noise on the track. To my mind that's a real nit-picker of a complaint.

These skis are available in both wood and the more durable fiberglass. My friend who finds X-C so possible loves her fish scales and wouldn't ski on anything else.

SKIS FOR WAXOPHILES

DON'T KNOCK WOOD: Among the X-C skis that you wax, wooden skis are the classic, the traditional, the skis for the purist. Here are the specifications for ideal wooden light touring skis.

1. They are laminated, rather than solid. The better ones have up to thirty-two laminations composed of many

and varied combinations of such woods as spruce, birch, beech, hickory, and balsa. Laminated skis are stronger, springier, more flexible, lighter weight, and keep their camber better than solid wood. They're also more expensive.

2. They have hickory soles. Racers prefer birch soles, because they are lighter and hold the wax better, but they are softer and less durable than hickory. For pleasure touring you need the additional toughness.

3. They have Lignostone edges. Contrary to its name, Lignostone is not mineral but vegetable—beechwood that has been compressed to one-seventh its original size and heated and impregnated with resins until it's seven times stronger than originally, yet still has the flexing characteristics of wood. It is a very durable substance and durability is what you want in a ski edge. Plastic edges are okay, but they damage more easily, are slightly more expensive, and they detract from the purity.

A peripheral reason for getting yourself a pair of classic boards is that before long they may go the way of the dinosaur and become collector's items suitable for hanging up for ski lodge decor. The supply of hickory—and all of it comes from the United States—is becoming insufficient to meet the needs of the burgeoning birthrate of ski tourers. On top of that, there are so many new nonwood developments in the cross-country ski line that the purist's delight may soon become obsolete. If manufacturers can get the performance of the synthetics up to their standard of durability, the end of the woods is here.

One other aspect of the purist's ski, the hickory bottom, is also sorely threatened. Some of the most tradition-bound Norwegian and Swedish manufacturers are furtively starting to slide a number of their skis out the door on plastic bottoms. These have the decided advantage of not having to be pine tarred. Partisans claim they wear better and even slide and glide better in certain wet conditions. Objectors say they don't hold the dry waxes as well, they demand repair more frequently than wood skis —and the repair is not the do-it-yourself project that pine tarring can be—and their cost is greater. Still, it's obvious that plastic bottoms are gaining on woods.

On your metal: The first year Fisher brought out its snappy metal touring ski the price was only $35, about the same price as a good wood. A knowledgeable shop attendant whispered in my ear that Fisher was selling them at a loss to hook the public and the following season the price would leap up. It is now the following season. Check him out.

You might also check out the skis themselves. I rented a pair of them for a week from the Wiiks' in Steamboat Springs and, although I started out whining for my old hickorys, by the end of the week I had adjusted and could see decided advantages to them, especially in terms of durability. There is nothing quite as dismal-making as snapping off a ski tip when you're out in the woods somewhere. Metals, virtually indestructible as they are, could save you from this. The bases of these skis are plastic with all the advantages and dis that that implies. My

Norwegian instructor said that to her surprise they held the wax very well. Her only complaint was that they tended to delaminate, but she said she thought that was only a "young sickness" which would be cured in the next year's model.

Original synthetics: Here's the future. When a popular sport emerges, can manufacturers with hot new products bearing high new price tags be far behind? No. They're breathing on us and in some cases it sounds more like greedy panting. Beware the startling breakthrough in some supersynthetic combinations of as many different substances as Edison used when he was trying to make the electric light bulb. The more expensive the end result, the more beware. Wait for the tests and reports and honest, unbiased evaluations—if you can find any—before you spring. Let someone else pay for the experiment. You can have all the fun you can handle on tried and true and less costly models.

Having a fit: Now that you're thoroughly confused over what kind of skis you want, I'll see if I can do the same for you with what length and stiffness to get. Just as in downhill, everyone has a different idea of the length you should have. A safe test, however, is to raise your arm above your head and choose a ski that hits between where your wrist meets your palm and your palm meets your fingers. If you are heavy and/or strong for your height, opt for the longer side of this measurement. If you're lightweight or light-strengthed, go for the shorter.

As for flexibility and its opposite, stiffness, your weight is a factor in your selection. The heavier you are, the stiffer should be your skis. If you're debating between several pairs of skis, place each pair bottom to bottom and squeeze the middles together with one hand. It's pretty easy then to separate the stiffs from the limps. Incidentally, you should be able to squeeze the skis together with one hand. If you can't make them meet without expending enough effort to burst a blood vessel in your neck, they're obviously too stiff for you.

If you want to fiddle around over your selection some more, you can stand on the skis in the place where the binding will be and see if your weight flattens them out, but not totally. Legend and song have it that you should still be able to pass something thin like a piece of paper under the middle. If you can't, they're too soft for you. If you can pass something thicker like a *Time* Magazine or a pastrami sandwich, they're probably too stiff. Incidentally, you might place the skis side by side on the floor and get down on your hands and knees and see if they both have the same camber—that is, they have the same amount of space under the center. Good quality skis almost always match perfectly, but it doesn't hurt to check and it makes you look very pro and as if you knew a lot about ski selection.

The very best and most accurate of tests of whether or not your skis are of the right stiffness is to go out and ski on them for a season and see where you make worn spots. If only the tips and tail wear, the skis are too stiff. If only the middle wears, they're too soft. There's just one problem with this very best and most accurate of tests. When you find out, it's too late to do anything about it.

A BETTER RAT TRAP: Bindings are the metal devices that attach your boots to your skis. Since skis are ordinarily sold without them, you have to choose the style and brand you want and have them mounted in the proper position on the ski. Most shops charge about five dollars a pair to do this job for you and they want to have your boots while they're doing it.

Basically, there are two kinds of bindings for Nordic skiing—cable and clamp. Cable bindings anchor the toe and have a cable that winds back around the heel. Cables are used with mountaineering skis and with above-the-ankle boots. Don't get cable bindings.

Clamp bindings, which anchor only the toe of the boot and leave the heel totally free, are what you need for light touring. In Sweden, where they were invented, the most popular brand is Rottefella, which translates as "rat trap." This clamp style permits you to move your boot up and down but not sideways.

To make the boot really secure and immovable, most clamp bindings have three or four vertical pins about a quarter of an inch high. (That's why clamp bindings are also called pin bindings.) These are matched to holes drilled in the sole of the boot. You step into these bindings, fitting the pins into the boot holes, and then you push down on the clamp and lock it in place. Some clamp bindings can be locked and released with a ski pole. Some of the better known brands are Rottefella, Snabb,

Karhu Kilpa, Villom, Troll, Jofa VM, Hope Rat Trap, and ABC Pin.

Should you get three or four pin bindings? It really doesn't matter. Often you have no choice, because the shop stocks only one kind. If you do have a choice, I'd go for the three pin. The reason I'd go for three pin is that I *went* for four pin. And now whenever I'm in a resort where I've taken my boots and want to rent skis, I inevitably find all they have are three pin; so I have to rent boots as well.

Lots of manufacturers are now coming out with pinless and step-in bindings with special designs, many of which fit only boots with matching plates, clips, or stops. I've heard that with some of these innovations the boot plate can work loose and leave you stranded out in the beauties of nature with no way to glide home. Since the advantages of these newer systems are not all that great, better to stick with the rat traps until the Mickey Mouse models get the flaws worked out.

An important adjunct to the bindings is a heel popper or heel plate. The popper is a rubber piece that fits on the ski where the heel meets it and prevents snow from building up. The plate, which may be plastic or rubber with steel, has serrated edges which help keep the heel from slipping off the ski. This is a formidable advantage in making turns; and I strongly advise the plate, especially since you can attach it yourself with the little nails that are provided, and it costs under a dollar.

When I bought my skis they installed a rubber popper on them. The second season around I became aware of the serrated plates, which the racers always use; so I pried off the popper and threw it into the trash and hammered on the plate. Not long afterward I noticed some skiers with the rubber popper right behind the toe clamp and the plate under the heel in addition. This combination gives you turning power *and* keeps the snow from building up uncomfortably under the ball of the foot and the instep. (Give snow the slightest opportunity and it will build up anywhere it can.)

THESE BOOTS WERE MADE FOR GLIDING: Of the total X-C equipment arsenal, I like the boots best. No, like is too mild a word; I adore everything about the boots—their square toes, their supple leather tops, their soft rolled snow cuff at the ankle, their snug heel, and their almost floating lightweightedness. I can ski or walk in them all day and still hate to take them off at night.

Not that I haven't had boot trouble, but only what I brought on myself by a stupid initial purchase. My instincts were not totally wrong. At least, I bought my first pair in the Italian Alps—in Val Gardena—where I knew I'd be getting the craftsmanship of the best bootmakers in the world. But I made two fatal errors: I bought my boots too large (that's not difficult to do when you wear size 4B) and I bought them with leather soles.

Even with the two pairs of socks worn for X-C (thin inners and thick outers), my boots were too roomy and gave me a loss of control—and with the unattached heel you don't have a heckuva lot left to lose. I tried to make them fit by wearing two heavy pairs of socks, but this merely cramped my toes so that I couldn't wiggle them and consequently they tended to turn to ice.

The leather soles soaked up water and in no time at all the toes were curled up almost as much as my ski tips, and the binding holes had deteriorated into jagged caverns. So if you know anyone who wears a European size 36 and doesn't mind soggy, curled soles, they can have a pair for mailing costs.

My second pair of boots I shopped for with extreme and excessive care. I took with me the two pairs of socks I intended to be wearing while skiing in order to fit the boots to my feet with the exact padding they would have on the trail. And I insisted on plastic molded soles (injected molded polyurethane) with leather tops—the ideal combination, because the plastic soles are waterproof and retain their shape and the leather uppers are flexible and allow the feet to breathe. Go thou and do likewise. Some Scandinavian boots are constructed totally of rubber, but for people with normal sweat glands these are like skiing in a sauna. All-plastic boots have a similar problem.

Since X-C boots are mainly imported, they are often marked with European sizes. There's a conversion chart in the Appendix in case the shop doesn't have one.

X-C boots come in all shapes, colors, and prices. For fun skiing there's only one shape—those that are cut just below the ankle. The over-the-ankle variety aren't that much warmer or drier and they *are* that much heavier. (Remember the old truism: a pound on the feet is like five on the back.) Black is the most common color, but some brands feature white, natural, brown, blue, and red.

Boots range in price from around $27 for Falk, Alfa, Norge, Skilom, et cetera, up to the Rolls-Royce of boots, Norrona, at close to $45.

Exploring the poles: Poles for X-C are lighter and longer than poles for downhill, and the baskets are larger. The usual Scandinavian-in-the-track variety is made of bamboo or Tonkin, a superstrong bamboo. Poles are also available in fiberglass and metal, but these are mostly for racers. Only if you're an inveterate pole-snapper would you need to spend the extra money on aluminum.

The main features to look for when purchasing poles are an adjustable strap so you can adjust it to have a good fit when you alternate from padded mittens to gloves and a cork or suede handle. When you notice that all the points of the X-C poles are bent, don't think they were all damaged in shipment. On the contrary, if they were *straight*, it would mean something had gone wrong. They are curved so they will slip out of the snow more easily after you've glided beyond them.

The length of the pole is a crucial factor for ease of skiing. To get a proper fit, just tuck the pole under your armpit. If it runs from armpit to floor—or even a little longer—it's the right size.

WARNING

Actually this warning is more of an anti-warning. Don't chew your cuticle and generate stomach acid and stay awake at night over picking out your X-C equipment.

Naturally, you want to get the best your money can buy and you don't want to get anything that will spoil your fun, but X-C equipment for the recreational skier is just not that critical. For example, my skis are a little too long and too stiff for my height and weight and strength, but even with this equipment error I can kick and glide along at a decent pace and make turns with no trouble. And even when I had my ill-fitting leather-bottomed boots with the chewed-up pin holes, I always had a glorious time.

So relax. Don't try to make a simple sport complex by sweating over the equipment. And don't worry if every item isn't exactly right. Be like the Oriental rug makers, who always weave in a little mistake, because they don't want perfection for fear of angering Allah.

3. DOING IT

A DOWNHILL skier friend of mine shuddered when he heard that I was taking up X-C. "But it's so much work!" No, it isn't, not if you do it right. Cross-country is the original easy-does-it sport. Your main goal should be to eliminate effort. The whole purpose behind learning to do it right is to develop that relaxed, rhythmic kick-glide, kick-gliide, kick-gliiiiide. And the more i's you can get into your glide, the better.

Cross-country is sometimes described as "walking on skis." That's wrong. It is *gliding* on skis. This glide is your free ride, and it's what makes ski touring the delectable experience it is. Let us begin.

THE LOWDOWN FOR DOWNHILLERS: The best way to learn downhill skiing is to learn cross-country first—and vice versa. The way you did it, the vice versa way is doing it the hard way. It's something like studying Latin to learn English grammar. But you've already been through the tough part, the downhill. Now, it should be nothing but smooth gliding.

You know what it feels like to be on skis. You've developed your sense of balance and improved your coordination and strengthened your legs. You also have already acquired a number of skills that you can transfer over to X-C: the kick turn, the sidestep, the herringbone, the snowplow, and the stem christie. This last is not an X-C basic, but it could come in handy. Some people have even been known to wedel on X-C skis.

You also have a couple of things to unlearn. The first of these is that your heel is fastened down, because it won't be in X-C. I've seen downhill converts, myself among them, spend their initial days on X-C skis stomping around flatfooted, because in their kinesthetic minds they still don't realize that they can raise their heels. This wipes out all the ease of X-C skiing and louses up your kick and glide. In fact, it louses up everything.

Later on when you come to a downhill stretch you may again forget that your heel is not clamped to the ski and also forget that you don't have steel on the edges of your skis. Consequently, you may try to do a few fast and furious and sharp turns in the Alpine manner. Splat.

The other thing that you have to unlearn should be easy for you. You have to go back to doing the natural thing. You can once again make the movements your body has always made in walking and running. No more must you twist your body into strange contortions. No more must you throw your weight in exactly the opposite place from where all your fibers cry out that it should be. With X-C you can go home again and achieve President Harding's great goal of normalcy.

On top of everything else, you can sigh a sigh of relief that a tremendous burden has been lifted from you—your cumbersome, leaden Alpine equipment. As Jeanne Parry, Scandinavian Airlines X-C advocate, puts it, "Lose sixteen pounds of ugly weight. Ski Nordic."

A LESSON IS MORE: It is obvious that the best way to learn how to X-C ski is to take a good lesson from a good instructor. Nothing matches watching a real live human being go through the motions for you and then having him check you out as you go through them. It is also a faster way to get through those odious beginning stages of clunking around awkwardly and wasting motion and energy before you break through to the fields of fun beyond.

But it may not be easy for you to find a good lesson. You may not live near a ski area that has X-C instruction, and perhaps you don't have the wherewithal in time or money to get yourself to one. Or you may get yourself to an area and find to your sorrow that the instruction is something less than good. This can happen in these early days of X-C popularity. As Ben Rinaldo, publisher of *Southwest Skier,* put it, "Cross-country schools are springing up all across the country like waterbed establishments," and, as I have discovered, a lot of them don't hold water. Many are just jumping on the bandwagon of a growing sport. Some of the instructors have just gone through a crash course and their teaching methods got a little mangled in the process.

My very first lesson was a good example. It took place in Switzerland and it went something like this.

We assembled in the waxing room, where our instructor, a taciturn type, lectured and demonstrated the technique of waxing the skis. As he worked over the skis, I had a chance to look over the class. It was not large. There were only the three of us Americans, a young Swiss couple of indeterminate marital status, a rather paunchy middle-aged Swiss, who might have been a grocer, and an extremely dapper, prematurely gray German, who appeared to be in his mid-thirties.

As the instructor finished waxing each pair of skis, he put them out through the window and leaned them against the building to cool. When they were all done, we trooped out the door, picked up our skis, and headed for the cross-country track.

"So," said the instructor, "we now put on our skis and to warm up"—he extended his pole and pointed—"we go to that little hill just on the other side of the bridge." I looked and then looked again, grateful that I was wearing my prescription sunglasses. That little hill just on the other side of the bridge was a good three-fourths of a mile away. Oh, well, since he hadn't even shown us how to do what we were supposed to be doing, this would no doubt be a leisurely trip.

I bent over to fasten the bindings on my skis and when

I straightened up, all the rest of the class, except for us three Americans, were in the track. By the time we managed to step around into position, they were off and running.

I was first in line of the three of us, so, clutching my poles hard enough to permanently embed my fingerprints in the handles, I pushed off and in no time at all had established a regular rhythmic pattern: gasp, gasp, strain, wheeze, semi-stumble, slip back . . . As it so often happens in sports, the harder you try, the more tense you become and the worse you perform. Before I even reached the bridge, sweat was trickling into my eyes, my turtleneck was sticking to the small of my back, and the marrow in my long bones was replaced with lead. The Swiss and German members of the class, striding smoothly along the track, became smaller and smaller as they gradually increased the distance between us from the size of a tennis court to a hockey rink to a football field.

Gasp, gasp, strain, wheeze, semi-stumble, slip back; gasp, gasp . . . This sport had all the fun and exhilaration of overtime in the coal mines or around the Horn in a galley ship . . . Gasp, gasp . . .

We finally caught up with the class just as the instructor was finishing an involved lecture on technique. Since he was giving the lecture in Schweitzer Deutsch, a Swiss dialect of German, we felt we hadn't really missed anything. He sent the rest of the class on a circle tour while he revealed a few fundamentals to us in English. I tried to concentrate on what he was saying. "Hold the poles loosely. Push down on the straps." "Keep the arms close to your sides." But it was a little disconcerting to see our classmates skimming around us as if on rails.

After our brief lecture, which hardly gave us a chance to gulp down a few breaths, the instructor sighted another distant point on the trail and off we went. Or rather off he and they went. The three of us fumbled into the track and sloshed ineptly in their wake.

Again we arrived wheezing and puffing just as the lecture was ending. The dapper German, who, among his other talents, spoke perfect English, flashed his even white teeth and welcomed us with, "Ah, here comes the 'Spirit of '76.' " And indeed we looked a great deal like the legendary battered trio. I personally felt as though I'd caught a musket ball in each calf.

I later found out that everybody else in the class but us had had miles of X-C touring under his boards. The German, for example, told us later that he had only taken the class to get acquainted with the instructor, an Olympic alternate, because he was going to try to talk him into letting him go out with him on his training sessions.

In another less-than-great lesson of mine the genuine, authentic, blond, accented Scandinavian Nordic instructors were off somewhere promoting their "outstanding ski touring program," leaving an electrician who moonlighted weekends teaching—so to speak—X-C. His teaching consisted of leading our mixed-ability class up a trail and shouting occasional tips over our heads, such as, "Never take your skis off the snow" and "sixty percent of your forward motion comes from your poles." (This latter tip, is, incidentally, dead wrong, at least for nonracers.

Your arms should supply only a tenth to a quarter of your forward power.)

And a friend wrote me another little X-C lesson horror story: "After a mere hour with the guy who heads the school, he tossed me into a night tour. Yep, at night. In the dark. With miner's lanterns strapped to our perspiring brows. And all uphill yet! We climbed almost a thousand feet to the top of a ridge overlooking the town. Almost killed me. You think you lagged behind your Swiss. They virtually had a posse dragging poor old me up the damned mountain. Finally made it without a heart attack. The down-ski was sort of fun. More so when my lantern's batteries went sour and I was skiing in the mere glow of less than a burning cigarette."

THE BAD AND THE BEAUTIFUL: By comparing the bad lessons and the superb ones, I've made a little list to help you distinguish between the two.

1. Look for an X-C school that's been in operation for at least two years, or, as in the case of Mt. Telemark in Wisconsin, a new one that has been set up by a bona fide Nordic expert—in this case, Sven Wiik, who is the bona fidest in the country.

2. Be sure that in their classes they separate those who have never done any skiing at all from those with downhill skiing experience. Otherwise, the lesson will be too hard and fast for the nonskiers and too time-wasting and boring for the skiers.

3. The best methods I've seen give you a first lesson on

a flat track to teach you the basics, followed by a brief, easy tour to tramp down the learning. The next lesson should teach you descending, climbing, and turns, followed again by a short tour to put it all in practice. Just saying, "Follow me," and letting you struggle along behind is *not* a lesson.

4. For those who use skis that need to be waxed, the principles of waxing should be included in the lesson, preferably with the instructor demonstrating and then with each student waxing his own.

5. The lesson should not be agonizing or frightening or exhausting. You should never have that "I'm not going to make it" feeling. The best lessons I've had, that is, the ones in which I learned the most, were the easiest and the most pleasant and the least strenuous.

If you have well-taught, all-coverage lessons, two are the most you need. Forever. A sound pair of lessons will give you lots of exercises and skills to practice on your own. Practice on your own is what it takes. Good balance and coordination only come after many an hour on the lean boards.

Naturally, if you decide to go into some phase of X-C more seriously, you'll want more coaching, but two for the fun of it are enough.

DOING IT YOURSELF: Unlike many sports, and that inevitable comparison with downhill again raises its hoary head, you *can* teach yourself X-C. All it takes is snow, skis, a minimum level of literacy, and a good measure of enthusiasm. A friend who also wants to learn X-C is a big help. You can criticize each other. After all, what else are friends for?

The following step by step is the step by step I have taken and taken and taken. I have had lessons from a Norwegian, a Swede, an Eastern American, a Western American, a very Northwestern American (his previous bailiwick was Alaska), and a Swiss who got his training in Canada. One of my instructors—one of the best—was a woman. Not only that, but she was a woman head of a cross-country ski school.

I kept taking the beginning and intermediate lessons over and over with different instructors. The instructions given here are a composite of the best ideas and suggestions and techniques of the best of the instructors I encountered.

FLAT TRACK BASICS

ON THE RIGHT TRACK: Seek out a flat open space and make yourself a training track by shuffling along with your skis about as far apart as your shoulders, until you've made a two-lane (one for each ski) oval about the size of a basketball court, or longer if you have the space. A prepared track makes gliding much easier, and at the beginning you want everything as easy as possible. Come to think of it, if you have good sense, you'll always want everything as easy as possible.

If the snow is deep, you'll probably also want to shuffle a track on either side of the original one. This will make poling easier, because you'll be poling in snow the same level as that you're skiing on. Your poles will also slip in and out more easily.

TAKE A BABY STEP: The first step is to get the feel of your skis and the feel of the motion of the basic technique of cross-country. Put your poles aside and go around the track slowly, scooting first one ski and then the other, gliding on the forward ski and letting the other one drag behind you at the end of a fairly straight extended leg. The motion is similar to skating, either ice or roller. Your weight is on the ski you're gliding on, and it should be solidly placed on a flat foot, not teetering on the ball of the foot or toes.

Neither ski ever leaves the snow. Keep your neck and shoulders relaxed, and this will tend to relax your whole body. Let yourself almost melt into a loose round-shoulderedness. If you've ever seen cross-country racers, they're usually lanky, stoop-shouldered types. (Chicken and egg question: Are they stoop-shouldered from racing in that position or are they good racers because of their body type?)

Forget your arms for now. Let them do what they will, and they will do the right thing. Don't rush it. Just scoot along at a comfortable pace until you begin to feel natural doing it. This shouldn't take long, because it is a totally natural movement.

DOING THE GROUCHO GLIDE: Now comes a little unnatural exaggeration. This is an exercise for strengthening legs. You can tuck it into your reticule and use it for practice sessions all your touring days. I call it the

Groucho Glide, because, except for the absence of the mustache, eyebrows, cigar, and leer, Groucho Marx is exactly whom you look like when you do it.

Remember how Groucho always walks in in semicrouch with his knees deeply bent, yet his back held straight? Do that on your skis, incorporating the glide of the first exercise and keeping the leg that is back extended as before. Be sure your head is moving along smoothly always on the same level—even as Groucho's—no bobbing or ducking. Keep looking straight ahead to where you're going, *not* down at your ski tips. Never look at your ski tips, unless you have your skis off and are inspecting them for damage.

Do this exaggerated knee bend, the Groucho Glide, until your legs begin to feel it. This may not take too long, since you'll be demanding a lot from muscles that usually have little asked of them in your daily life.

Knee Note: In this exercise what you're really doing is a supercolossal, exaggerated knee bend. What you should be doing all the time in X-C is what will seem to you to be an exaggerated knee bend. A rule of knee is that, when you're skiing properly, your knees will always feel twice as bent as they really are. When you think your knees are slightly bent, they're probably as straight as your ski poles. Always try to ski with the feeling that your knees are bent way too much. Then they'll probably be bent just right.

PRESENT ARMS: Now for a little coordination workout, still without poles. This time the arms get their exaggerated action. With your legs going back to the more normal skating motion and without any Grouchoization, swing your arms naturally . . . but unnaturally. What I mean by this is the right arm should swing forward when the left leg goes forward and vice versa in the natural way your arms swing when you walk. Yet it is unnatural, because in this exercise you swing them much, much farther. When you swing your arm forward, swing it straight forward, unbent, until it is shoulder high. You should really feel this in the muscles in the back of your arm.

In this exercise you'll have your first opportunity to experience that phenomenon that when you stop to think about a perfectly normal everyday movement, you get all bollixed up and can't do it any more. Actors have found that when they are asked to "just walk across the stage" they suddenly discover that they don't know which arm goes forward with which leg, and they wind up stumbling around, as if they were victims of some strange nerve and muscle disease. You too may find that when you start concentrating on arm movements, they get completely out of sync with your legs. You're thinking too much. It's like X. J. Kennedy's verse on writing poetry:

ARS POETICA

The goose that laid the golden egg
Died looking up its crotch;
To find out how its sphincter worked,
Would you lay well? Don't watch.

You could paraphrase Kennedy's last line with, Would you ski well? Don't watch! Not meaning, of course, that you shouldn't look where you're going and run into trees and fall over cliffs, but, rather, don't concentrate so hard on your body movements that you can't make them.

When you do find yourself hopelessly out of whack, just stop. Stand erect. Then, shuffle off slowly as if walking, letting the arms do what they will. Then gradually stretch out into your glide and you should be back in order again.

Another important thing to remember about the arms is to keep them close to the body as you swing them. This not only eliminates wasted motion, but it will give you a lot more strength when you start using your poles. Perhaps it will help if you try to imagine that you're carrying a heavy bucket of sand in each hand. Under those circumstances you'd never be holding your arms way out to the side.

Balancing act: This exercise is designed to help you build up your balance on the skinny skis. It may prove to be the hardest of the exercises and one you'll need to practice over and over while you're first learning.

Go back to the original relaxed skating that you did at first. Nothing exaggerated. Now, when you're in the glide, lift the tail of the ski you're not gliding on off the snow. This will insure that you have *all* your weight on the gliding ski, where it belongs. When you reach the point that you can do this exercise on either ski without teetering and near-toppling, you'll know that balance is no longer a problem Don't expect this to happen during the first day or the first week or even the first month or year you're on X-C skis.

Poles apart: Now it's time to bring the long-neglected poles into the picture. Lift the strap so that it forms a right angle with the pole. Reach up through the strap, then grasp both pole and strap. The strap will be between your thumb and first finger. (See diagrams.) Grasp, however, may be too strong a word. You should always hold the pole loosely. There is nothing that will tense up the whole body as thoroughly as a death grip on the

The Pole Grip in the Push

poles. If you play tennis or golf, think what a desperate clutching of the club or racket does to your game.

Actually, when you plant the pole and push with it, you are—or should be—pushing more on the strap than pole itself, because your grip is so loose. And when you stretch the pole straight out behind you during your glide, you should be holding it with only your thumb and first two fingers.

Where and when to plant the pole will work itself out,

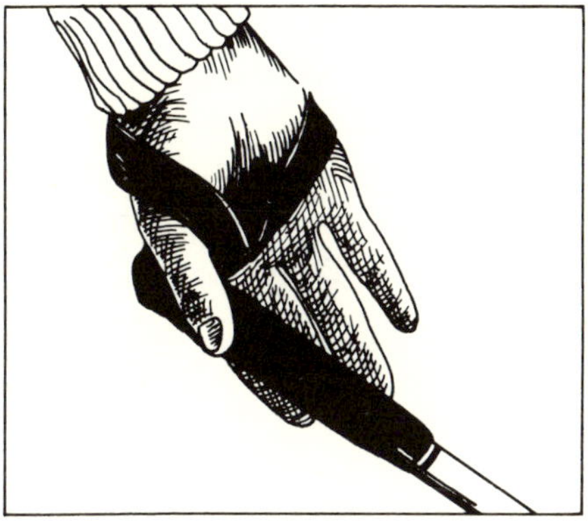

The Pole Grip in the Glide

if you let nature take its course. Just remember not to plant it way out to the side or way out in front. It goes just a little ahead of your forward boot (which is on the opposite side of the hand you're poling with). It goes into the snow at about the time you push off into your glide, because it's helping you get a good, hearty forward motion. Consequently, be sure you really use your pole. Dig it in. Don't, as one instructor accused me of doing, "just use the pole for decoration," pecking lightly at the snow.

THE DIAGONAL STRIDE: Now we're ready to put it all together and do the real thing, the diagonal stride. The term diagonal stride strikes up a vision, at least in my mind, of the kind of on-the-bias trot that dogs do. The diagonal stride in X-C, on the contrary, carries you straight forward. The diagonal bit comes in with the body position. The right arm goes forward as the right leg goes back and vice versa, just as in walking.

The diagonal stride is the basic cross-country stride. It's what you'll be doing more than anything else in ski touring. Therefore, it might be wise to follow the admonition of Mignon McLaughlin in her *Neurotic's Notebook:* "If you have to do it every day, for God's sake learn to do it well."

Practice the diagonal stride with poles, trying to achieve that magic moment when you suddenly feel the

The Diagonal Stride

rhythm as it all comes together. Kick and pole, glide; kick and pole, glide; kick and pole, glide. The first time you hit the rhythm, you'll probably fall apart on the next step out of sheer surprise and joy at your success. (Also, you tend to forget to breathe while it's going on and you suddenly find yourself running out of that vital life commodity.) Still, once you've felt it, you know what it is you're striving for, what, in fact, X-C is all about, and it will keep getting easier and easier to find, until you have that beautiful rhythm all the time.

For kicks: A great deal is made of the kick in cross-country skiing. The kick is the push you give from one foot to get you going on the glide on the other. It is probably the greatest point of confusion in cross-country technique. The name is the first problem. When most of us think kick and not the kind of forward thing field goal kickers or can-can choruses do, then we think of a backwards kick like that done by a donkey. But if you try to do one of these donkey kicks on X-C skis, almost invariably your foot slips and you get thrown off your stride.

Some instructors counsel you to think of the kick as the same motion you'd use when riding a scooter. This is just as befuddling and befouling of the stride as the donkey version.

The best suggestion I've heard from an instructor is, "Forget about the kick." I'd actually already started forgetting about it on my own, but I was having terrible guilt feelings until he told me to forget it.

SING ALONG WITH X-C: One instructor reported to a class I was taking that she once had a student who found it easier to get into the rhythm of the stride if he hummed under his breath. "What did he hum?" we all chorused, looking for an easy key to success. In this case, it turned out to be a Francis Scott Key to success, because what he hummed was "The Star-Spangled Banner."

Song selection aside, the anthemizer did have a good idea. Humming or singing can help you hang onto your rhythm. And *your* rhythm it must be. Each of us has his own internal metronome. We range from largo to presto and cover all stops in between. You'll find yourself naturally falling into the rhythm that suits you best. When you do, match your song to it. Whether it be "Old Man

River" or "Holiday for Strings," the song is you, and that's what counts.

HANDPOWER: After you've practiced the diagonal stride for a while and feel you have the basic idea, here's a way to get a little more pow into it.

Up to now you've probably been letting your feet and legs set the pace, and the arms have just gone along with the rhythm. Now reverse the process. Think hands, or, rather, fists. Try to get the feeling that all your power is concentrated in those fists, and wham them hard back and forth. Let them set the pace. Forget feet. You should still be driving with your knees, but the hands are in charge.

Changing the focus of your attention like this, I found, is a great way to get the sluggishness out of your stride.

DOUBLE POLING: This is a complex-sounding name for the simplest and most natural of maneuvers on X-C skis. Double poling is swinging both your poles way up and out in front of you at the same time, then planting them with a powerful thrust, while simultaneously sinking into a deep knee bend with both skis parallel. You push on the

Double Poling

poles with all might and main. As you shoot forward in a long power glide, you gradually rise from the depth of your deep knee bend. At the same time, your poles go straight back and up behind you. To get a good snap with your poles, try to hit your hands together behind your back. (You won't make it, but just to try will get your arms back where they belong.)

To be able to double pole with no trouble, all you really need is to see it done once. In fact, some people who have never seen it done invent it for themselves. It's that easy and that natural.

You can use double poling to provide a little respite from the diagonal stride. Anything you keep doing over and over gets tiring after a while. A break in the pattern gives the body a chance to relax. Double poling is also good for getting up speed going downhill.

DOUBLE POLING WITH KICK: This is hard to do, because it's tough to get the rhythm right, and if the rhythm's wrong, you emerge looking and feeling like a stumblebum. But when it's right, ah, there's nothing like it. You look and feel like a champion.

The pros use this stride a lot in races, and if you've watched X-C racing in movies or on TV, you've undoubtedly observed the double pole with kick. And I hope you have seen it, because it's almost impossible to do, if you haven't. And at first it's still pretty hard to do, even if you have.

What happens is this. You're going along with your old reliable diagonal stride, and it occurs to you to do a spot of D-P w/k; so you swing your fists forward and up high, as if supplicating the Gods. Then you plant your poles with force and drama, and at the exact moment you plant them, you kick off with your second favorite foot, lifting the tail off the track. This gives you a powerful glide on your favorite foot. Both arms snap back behind you, as in straight double poling.

If you want to repeat this ego hype of a stride, just bring the kicked back ski up next to the gliding one, as

Double Poling with Kick

you raise your arms for the next spectacular double pole plant. And so it goes. When you've done it once and caught the rhythm, it's easier to find it again. You can use the double pole with kick for much the same purposes as the plain double pole, and also for when you just want to show off a bit.

SWEDISH TWO-STEP: I call this the Swedish two-step, because I learned it from Hans Wiik (Sven's nephew). He called it just the "two-step," but said he didn't like this name for it. He told us it is neither accurate nor descriptive, and he's right. Mainly, it's a way to rest your arms when you're on a long, rather vigorous tour. It's used with the standard diagonal stride. It is, in fact, two diagonal strides planting poles followed by two strides without planting poles. (When you don't plant your poles, you must let your arms swing naturally, holding your poles above the snow.) The rhythm of it is pole-pole, glide-glide, pole-pole, glide-glide. Easy and very restful for tightened-up triceps.

KICK TURN: Before you leave the flat, it's a good idea to learn and practice a maneuver you'll be using later on hills: the kick turn. This is harder than it looks when you see an expert do it, yet easier than it seems the first time you try it.

Stand with your skis parallel and fairly close together. Twist your upper body around so that it is facing to the side. Plant both your poles firmly behind your skis with your arms straight out to the sides. Leaning on your poles, kick the ski that's in the direction you're facing straight up, tail down in the snow. Make sure the tail is just barely resting on the snow. If you dig it in, you're going to have a heck of a time getting it out again.

Turn the up-kicked ski around and place it alongside the other ski, only going in the opposite direction. (Harder done than said.) Now, put your weight totally on the newly turned ski and bring the other ski over, around, and beside it. You'll need to bring your pole around with the ski to help in the balancing act.

When you do this musculo-obscenity on a hill, lest your skis slide out from under you, *always* be sure your skis

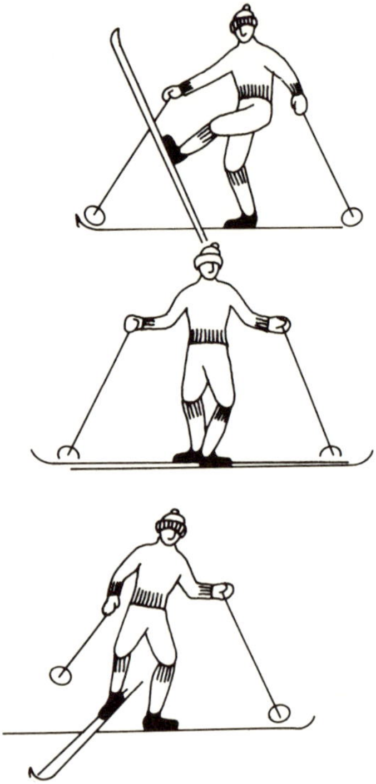

Kick Turn to the Left

are across the fall line. (The fall line is the most direct route straight down the hill—the way a snowball or a body would roll.) Another always with the kick turn is when you twist and face, always twist and face downhill. If you don't understand why, try facing uphill, but try it on a not-very-steep hill.

One more caution in doing kick turns on hills. When you turn the downhill ski in the opposite direction, be certain it's exactly parallel to the other ski. If it's pointed even slightly downhillward, when you put your weight on it, nature will take its downhill course, and you'll have no choice but to go along with it.

AFTER THE FALL: Many X-C classes make a big deal out of falling down and getting up the right way. Admittedly, it is best if you have the presence of mind to fall sideways or backwards rather than headfirst into the snow, but in my experience you often don't have any choice.

As for getting up after a fall, classes really get involved in the complexities of this one. One of my rawest new recruits told me after her first lesson that getting up after a fall was her biggest problem. The instructor explained very carefully how to twist around and get both your skis parallel on the same side and then how to take both poles together and plant the points in the snow and hoist yourself up gracefully with them. Unless, of course, you were in deep snow, in which case you were to lay the poles on the snow in an X position and then place your hand in the middle of the X and push yourself up.

As to be expected, the raw recruit fell. Since she was trying to remember all these complex directions, it took her about ten minutes to struggle up. The next time, she vowed to herself, if the instructor wasn't looking, she'd "just get up." She fell again. The instructor wasn't looking. She "just got up" in about thirty seconds. So if you can just get up, by all means do so. You only have to resort to all those other machinations for getting up if you find just getting up doesn't work.

CLIMBING, DESCENDING, TURNING

Now it's time to head for the hills or, at least, a hill, a very small and shallow and manageable one on which to learn the things you have to do when you run across a hill when you're out touring. If the snow is fresh and/or deep, you should tramp around and compact it in the area where you're going to be doing your exercises. When you're learning something new, you don't need the additional complication of deep snow to stumble in.

Climbing

TACKING: The basic principle in climbing, as in all X-C, is to do it in the easiest, most effortless way possible. The longer, steadier pace is usually preferable to the Teddy Roosevelt charging up San Juan Hill method.

The very easiest kind of climbing is sometimes called tacking. It is simply zigzagging back and forth across the hill in a slightly upward direction, using a kick turn each time you want to get yourself started in the opposite direction. The best line up the hill is the one that feels best for you. Some people prefer a steeper route, others a shallower one. If it feels good, do it.

THE STOMP OF APPROVAL: On not too steep slopes you can go straight up, using your old faithful diagonal stride with slight variations. Shorten your stride, bend your knees more (but still keep your back straight), and have "heavy boots," that is to say, really press them in hard, as if you were wearing diving boots. I personally also find it sometimes helps if I think of myself as jogging up the hill.

If you find yourself slipping backwards, then lift your skis off the snow and really stomp them down as you climb. Think of yourself as squashing a scorpion that threatens your life or, on a happier note, crushing grapes in a vintage year. Even with very poor technique and the

Straight up the Slope

wrong wax, you can usually make it up the hill with this stomping technique.

Incidentally, although you'll be using your poles in your climb, most of your power is—or should be—in your legs and feet. If you find yourself leaning too heavily on your poles, it's probably because you're unsure of your technique. ("So what else is new?" was my thought when this was pointed out to me in one of my early lessons.)

Herringbone: Another way straight up the hill is the herringbone, and a more clumsy, time-consuming method of ascension it would be hard to find. I think only its catchy name and the attractive pattern it makes in the snow have allowed it to survive. It is a duck-footed, toes-

Herringbone

out struggle up the hill with your skis making a  pattern, as you lean back on your poles and try to keep from toppling over or stepping on your own ski tails. The only time I ever do a herringbone is when I'm taking a lesson and they make me do it. You may like it. Stranger things have happened.

Sidestepping the issue: If a hill is truly steep and neither stomping nor herringboning do it for you, you have two choices:

1. You can forget about climbing that particular hill.
2. You can sidestep it.

The sidestep is easy, but slow and tiring. You stand on the hill with your skis as always across the fall line. Then, you lift the uphill ski and move it up the hill and plant it firmly, digging in your uphill edge as much as possible,

Sidestepping

remembering that X-C ski edges are not all that incisive. Next, move the downhill ski up beside the uphill ski, this time digging in the inside edge, and so on.

To get a little more travel for your effort in this climb, turn it into a forward sidestep by moving your uphill ski forward as well as up.

In all varieties of the sidestep be careful to get the tail of your ski up off the snow as you step. Otherwise, the tendency is to just lift the tips and leave the tails pointing downhill. This can cause a sudden, unplanned trip backwards down the hill.

Descending

Downhill all the way: What goes up must come down, and that's pretty nice, because going downhill is the easiest way to travel, as long as you don't turn it into a disastrous way to travel.

The easiest and safest method is tacking or traversing. Traversing is skiing across the hill perpendicular or almost perpendicular to the fall line. You go back and forth

The Schuss

across the hill in a slightly downward direction in the same leisurely way you may have come up.

If the hill is not too steep and not too long and has a good flat runout at the bottom, you can go straight down in a schuss. You do this by keeping your skis parallel about shoulder distance apart. You bend your knees, but you do *not* bend over at the waist. Keeping loose, you zap down the hill.

Whatever you do during the descent, don't throw all your weight forward, as you do in downhill schussing. With your loose heels, if you throw your weight forward, all is lost, especially your ability to remain upright. If anything, your weight should be ever so slightly back.

TELEMARK: The Telemark, named after the area in Norway where modern skis and bindings were invented, is the other show-offer in X-C. It's also fun to do. I don't mean the Telemark turn, which only an expert can do with aplomb, because modern X-C skis aren't long

The Telemark

enough to work well in this turn. (In the very early days of skiing when the Telemark turn was in flower, they actually skied with one long and one short ski.)

The Telemark *position,* however, is a good stable yet flashy way to go down the hill. In it you put your weight all—or virtually all—on one ski (choose your strongest leg for this job) and ride it with your knee very deeply bent, as deeply as in the Groucho Glide. The other unweighted ski is stretched out behind you with your leg as straight as you can get it without making it rigid.

The Telemark position is especially useful for going over bumps and through gullies. Splitting the skis in this way gives you more stability and reduces the risk of breaking your skis, because it helps you ride over the odd terrain rather than whamming both tips into a bump side or gully wall.

Snowplow: This is the position of all work in downhill skiing and the one everyone reverts to in moments of ter-

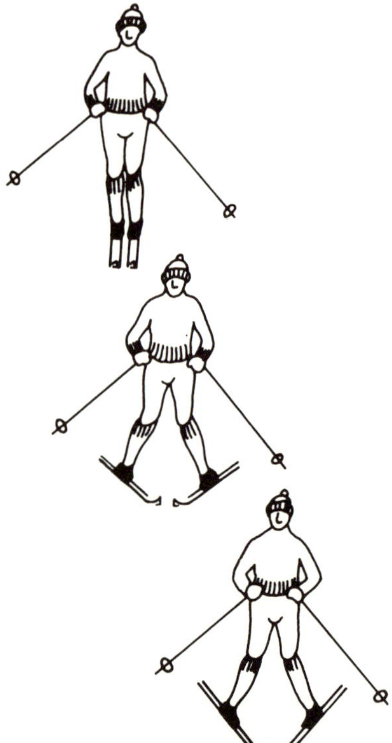

The Snowplow

ror and insecurity. It also has its uses in X-C, but fewer uses than in downhill. It's not good in a track and it's not good in unpacked snow and these two conditions are what you have most in touring.

In the snowplow you push out your tails so that the skis form a reverse V. (Be careful not to cross your tips.) This slows you down and by shifting your weight to one ski or the other, you can also make turns with the snowplow.

The Snowplow Turn

You will turn in the direction opposite to the ski you put your weight on. Weight on left ski, you'll turn right. Weight on right ski, you'll turn left.

HOW TO SKI DOWN AN ICY HILL: Bad news. You cannot ski down an icy hill on cross-country skis. Your edges are not steel and they are not sharp. They will neither hold in a traverse nor give you any kind of control in a turn.

To get down an icy hill on cross-country skis, take off the skis and walk down the hill to where there is either no more ice or no more hill.

Turning

One good turn: One good turn is all you need in X-C. This is a good thing, because one good turn is about all you have. It's the step turn or, as it is in its more advanced form, the skating turn. You do, of course, have the kick turn, but that's a stationary turn. The snowplow, as I just mentioned, has its limitations in terms of conditions. But the step turn can be used in almost all circumstances in most all conditions and at almost all speeds. The step turn falls into the basic category right there with the diagonal stride.

Since the step turn is such an important part of your arsenal of cross-country skills, it's worth spending time on some exercises to learn to do it the right way.

Going around in circles: The first exercise you do on the flat. Stand with your skis parallel. Then, leaving the heels of your skis in the same place, start stepping around in a circle by raising the tip of one ski and moving it to the side, then raising the tip of the other ski and bringing it beside the first. Keep doing this until you've made an entire circle. Your pattern in the snow will resemble a many-petaled daisy.

Now do the circle-stepping in the opposite direction. This moving of the tips to change direction is the core of the step turn.

No weight: The next exercise in building the step turn is to go back to your mini-hill and descend in the normal manner with skis parallel. As you go down, lift one ski off the snow and keep it there as long as possible. You can use your poles to help you balance. This method of lifting the ski off the snow is not quite the same as the lifting off you did on the flat track to develop balance. Balance is important here too, of course, but the main idea of this exercise is to get the *tip* of the ski, rather than the tail, off the snow. It's with the ski tip that you're going to be changing direction in the step turn.

When doing this exercise, be careful to return the ski gently to the snow. Don't slam it down or it may grab the snow, stop moving, and trip you up.

Practice this exercise several times, alternating lifted skis.

THE FIRST STEP: Okay, now you're ready for the real thing. Descend your small hill, step out with the toe of one ski, bring the other ski alongside it, and voilà, you've changed direction. If you haven't turned enough for your purposes, take another step and another and another, until you have. Many small steps are better and easier than one flip-you-out-of-balance giant one.

If you have trouble with this initial step turn, it's probably because you're approaching it too tentatively. This turn calls for decisive action. It has to be a total commitment. No hesitancy. Just as when you dive into a pool you can't leave one foot up on the board, when you step into this turn you have to throw all your weight onto the stepped-out ski and then all your weight on the other ski after you've brought it around so you're free to step out again with the original stepper.

Another point to remember is that you must keep moving through the turn. You don't stop and pick your way around in a gingerly manner and then start going forward again.

STEP LIVELY: After you've gotten the principle of the step turn, then you can start putting some pizzazz into it. First practice giving yourself a double pole push as you

The Advanced Step Turn or Skating Turn

make your first step. When that starts working well, make it a single pole push with the pole that is opposite to the stepping ski. This is then like doing a diagonal stride through the step turn.

Finally—and this may take a while—you should be skating snappily through the turn in sharp, decisive strides like Ard Schenk in the Olympics.

The Impossible Dream: Stopping

Now you know the basics. All except one, that is. You may have noticed that I've left out a very important skill, namely, how to stop. There's a reason for my sin of omission, one which I will now explain with a true life story.

After one cross-country ski lesson in Switzerland and another at Yosemite, I felt ready to ski a little on my own. I was staying at the Scandinavian Lodge in Steamboat Springs, Colorado, and I struck out one morning on one of Sven Wiik's marked trails through the woods. The trail had already been cut by other early-morning skiers. It was smooth skiing in good tracks.

Going away from the lodge, the route was mainly uphill, but my wax was right and I was full of breakfast energy and mountain air, so I chugged along at a fair clip. At the end of the trail I did a kick turn and started back. As it traditionally works out, that which is uphill going out is downhill coming back. This trail followed the old tradition. As I traveled down the trail, I started going faster and FASTER and *FASTER*.

During this accelerating descent it suddenly occurred to me that I had no idea how to stop. I had several ideas as to how I couldn't stop. I couldn't snowplow, because my skis were rocketing along well fastened to the trail rails created by the previous skiers. With no edges and those long floppy skis I knew an into-the-hill christie would be a disaster of splintered skis and maybe splintered me. At the speed I was going dragging my poles did nothing for me except make me worry that I might drop them.

A tree loomed. The trail turned just before it. I knew my momentum and lack of turning skill made an intimate encounter with the tree inevitable. I bailed out. Not wisely and not well. It was one of those headfirst dives that leaves you face-down, spread-eagled in the snow, looking like Leonardo da Vinci's drawing of the proportions of the human figure.

Since the snow was powder and deep and I was in the next thing to an impossible position to get out of, it was with much mighty flailing and wallowing and ultimate removing of skis that I finally struggled out and up. With snow melting down my neck and inside my boots and cuffs, I picked my way carefully and slowly down the rest of the trail home.

That afternoon I approached the resident Nordic instructor, deciding I could use another lesson. "What I'd really like to know," I said, grinning half-wittedly, "is how to stop. I know it sounds weird, but although I've had a couple of lessons, nobody has ever said much about stopping."

The instructor traced a pattern on the snow with his ski pole and coughed and cleared his throat. "Well . . . er . . . ah . . . you see, it's very complicated."

"Oh?" I said, bracing myself for a complex lecture on the principles of physics.

"The fact is . . . *you can't stop on cross-country skis!*" (Italics and exclamation point mine.) "Of course," he continued, "you can always stop by running into a tree. But you don't need a lesson for that."

I could not but agree. After all, I could have run into that tree out there on the trail with no instruction in the art at all. But he was a good instructor and kind and didn't leave it at that. He went on to explain one of the Great Truths of X-C: you should never get yourself into a situation where you have to do anything in a hurry—especially stopping—because on cross-country skis you *can't* do anything in a hurry—especially stopping. This is a cerebral sport. You have to think. You have to plan ahead. It's not like bashing a downhill piste on Alpine skis where you can, and often must, have split-second reactions and make movements so fast they blur.

Planning ahead in cross-country often involves not getting yourself going so fast that you can't stop without falling. But here's a heartening piece of news. While you can't stop on cross-country skis, you *can* slow down. There are several ways of doing this:

1. You can drag your poles behind you. If you're skiing a cut trail, drag them out in the untracked snow. This method unfortunately only works if you're already going so slowly that you hardly need to slow down at all.
2. If you have a certain amount of time and space for your maneuver, you can get yourself out of the fall line and heading uphill. A step turn will usually work for this.
3. You can do the old faithful snowplow, but in slow motion, please. Nothing precipitous. And beware: the snowplow can be risky in deep snow or on irregular terrain. If you are skiing in a track, you can do a half-snowplow, keeping one ski in the track and snowplowing the

other along the soft snow to the side.

4. If you're skiing a track, you can ski out of it into the softer snow. This will automatically slow you down. You can ski out of it, that is, if the track isn't so deeply cut that you run the risk of tripping yourself getting out of it and if you aren't skiing a trail through the woods—as I was—and there's no place to go except into a tree or bush.

The Side Brake

5. You can take the straps off your wrists and hold both poles with both hands, one hand gripping the grip and the other about halfway—or farther—down. You drag them to one side, pressing down on this brake as hard as you can.

6. Using the same grip and more agility, you can thrust the poles back between your legs and drag them there,

leaning your body weight into the effort. (Note: if you have lots of body weight and use bamboo poles, this may cause breaking as well as braking.)

7. You can sit down on your skis—actually it works out that you're sitting between your skis—and drag anchor. This is one of the most effective albeit least impressive methods.

When all these slowdowns fail, you must then fall. You have no choice. But don't do as I did. Make it a fall to the

The Between-the-Legs Brake

side instead of the head-first swan dive. A side fall is much safer both for you and for your skis and much, much easier to get up from without losing your dignity or your aridity.

There is also one way not to stop, besides running into a tree, that is. It is stabbing your poles in front of you as if you were making the kill in a bullfight. The natural tendency for poles thus stuck is to direct their handles straight at your soft underbelly. If you're moving along at a good rate of speed—and why else would you be taking such desperate measures to stop—you could be in for a double whammy that would do some rather serious intestine rearranging.

I don't mean for all this to sound grim and disturbing and make you nervous about X-C. It is really the safest of sports, if you pursue it sanely. Sane pursuit means checking your speed before you reach the point that you *have* to check your speed. It's as the Norwegians put it. Downhill skiing is like riding a bicycle without pedals. Cross-country is like riding a bicycle without brakes. Conduct yourself accordingly.

4. WAXING

WAXING serves three purposes in cross-country skiing: it protects the skis; it makes them slide in the glide; and it makes them grip in the climb. Correction: waxing serves *four* purposes. And the fourth may be the most important of all. It provides the sport of ski touring with a mystique, that certain esoteric, *je ne sais quoi* that gives the sport's practitioners something to ponder and argue over and experiment with and philosophize about; something to keep outsiders mystified and impressed when you're coming on strong with "special green" and "klister" and "Grundvalla" at cocktail parties.

Correction of the correction: there's also a fifth purpose for waxing. It gives us something to complain about. Complaints are vital to a sport, and X-C really has nothing else to grouse about. The equipment is comfortable and the skills are easy to acquire and execute. It's such a uniformly pleasant activity that it might lack bite and savor if it didn't have the irritation of waxing.

HOW WAX WORKS: When I was small, to me one of life's greatest mysteries was how does a thermos bottle know whether you want what you put into it to be kept cold or hot. A similar life mystery for adults to brood over is how does the wax know whether you want it to grip or glide? The answer involves a lot of physics, but translated for nonscientists by a nonscientist, it is: when you stomp your weight down, as you do in a climb or in the kick part of the diagonal stride, the wax grips. When the ski is unweighted or moving, the wax glides. Remember in the exercise for the step turn how you were cautioned *not* to stomp down suddenly on the ski you had just lifted? This was because, if you did, your wax would think you wanted it to grip and would proceed to do so.

Why wax grips at all is involved with the structure of the snow crystals and their moisture content. When snow first falls, the crystal structure is like that of the classic snowflakes that you see on Christmas cards. The flakes have lots of little sharp points sticking out in all directions. With all these little grabbers out ready to take hold, the crystals, especially if they're dry, don't need much to hold on to. Consequently, you use a hard wax. As the snowflakes age or begin to melt, their little points round off and their grabbing power diminishes. Then you need a softer wax for them to get a grip on.

After a period of melt and freeze, the snow becomes,

depending on the temperature, crusty, corny (a texture something like granulated sugar), or sloppy. In any of these conditions, the snow has virtually no grabbers left to hold on with. The wax has to provide a very soft, sticky helping hand. The wax designed to do this is called klister. Klisters come in fat tubes and have a consistency something like model airplane glue mixed with taffy apple coating.

The art of the matter lies in choosing a wax that is like the Baby Bear's bed in *Goldilocks*—not too hard and not too soft, but just right. If you choose a wax that's too hard, the grabbers can't grab when you try to climb and you slip backwards. If you choose one that's too soft, the grabbers will insist on grabbing when you want to glide. Your skis will "ice up" (really this should usually be called "snow up," because snow is stuck all over the bottom of the skis in a thick layer), making it impossible to glide and nearly impossible to move.

Breaking the color code: And then there's the story of the woman who goes into the ski shop for cross-country wax. "What color would you like?" asks the salesman.

"Oh, any color at all is fine with me," replies she amiably. "I like all colors."

But seriously, folks, you do not select X-C wax by picking out your favorite color or one that matches your eyes or knee socks. Cross-country waxes are color-keyed according to hardness. Five of the major brands—Swix, Rex, Rode, Ex-Lite, and Toko—have almost identical and almost interchangeable colors. They go from the cooler colors—green, blue, purple—for the harder waxes and into the warmer tones—red, yellow—for the softer waxes. Some of the other waxes—Bratlie, Vauhti—have their own unique color system. With klisters the color code starts all over again. A table of approximations and correspondings is given in the Appendix.

Some of the companies have developed a simple two-wax system for beginners. Bratlie's Tomm Murstad's Tur Pakning and Toko's Touring Plus and Touring Minus are examples. A new independent on the two-wax scene is Jack Rabbit wax concocted by Jack Rabbit Johannsen's son, who is a chemistry major graduate of McGill University. In all these systems the two waxes will supposedly handle your whole spectrum of waxing needs. But to use them effectively you have to know how thick to put them on, whether or not to smooth them out, etc. Some consider that all these decisions make the duo packs almost as tricky to use as the total wax rainbow.

Although the two-wax systems have distinct disadvantages, they are terrifically handy to have in your pack should snow conditions change on the trail or should your wax wear off. One red-klister day in Laurentides Park outside of Quebec I rented a pair of skis with yesterday's klister on them. Being basically lazy and disinclined to put on klister if I can possibly avoid it, I set off, assuming the leftovers would work.

About a mile out I lost my kick and my climb. If I hadn't had a bar of Jack Rabbit wet snow klister in my pack, the day would have been lost. I'll admit I had to stop and reapply the wax a couple of times, because it wore off faster than regular klister, but it certainly beat walking home with my skis on my shoulder instead of on my feet.

All the major wax brands are excellent products. Choose any one that's readily available. Personally, I use Rex for the valid reason that I won a free kit of it in a drawing at a Far West Ski Association touring meeting. It's less confusing to stick with one brand until you master it. Then you can branch out into clever and subtle combinations of brands. (See the Mountaincraft chart for Rocky Mountain snow in the Appendix.)

CHARTING YOUR COLOR: How are you to know what color wax to use when? The best way is to be staying at a resort or in a city like Oslo where X-C is a big thing and where they hang signs outside ski shops saying, "Blue wax today." If you're working on your own, it's a little more complicated.

You *could* just buy a wax kit containing a selection of waxes and klisters and when the moment of waxing truth comes, read the instructions on the containers. You *could* do this, but after spending some time reading wax and klister labels, I don't recommend it. Most waxes are manufactured in a foreign country and as far as the instructions are concerned, something is often lost in the translation. For example:

"For frash, little moist and falling snow at approximately 0° C."

"For newly fallen snow by thaw and slop weather."

"For fresch, fine grained snoy from −2° C. to −8° C."

"For dusty, hard, fine-grained snow at −8° C. and less."

"Both for newly-fallen and for old snow when small frost is changing to thaw."

Coupled with this little translation problem is the location of the English instructions on the wax containers. Since we English-speakers were the last ones to climb onto the X-C bandwagon, the English instructions are usually the ones printed closest to the top. Therefore, when you peel the lead foil of the container down as you use up the wax, the English instructions are the first to go. Out on the trail you wind up trying to read the Finnish or Norwegian instructions.

THE CHART OF THE MATTER: Luckily, wax charts are easy to come by. They're distributed by wax manufacturers and ski shops as freely as calendars around Christmastime. Also, every book on cross-country skiing—including this one; see Appendix—has at least one chart. It doesn't much matter which chart you use, as long as it makes a modicum of sense to you and covers the brand of wax you're using. When you find a chart you like, though, stick to it until you get really familiar with it so that before long you have it in your head. That's the best place to carry it, since then you're not too likely to leave it at home or to get klister all over it.

THROUGH THICK AND THIN: Even when you have a chart which you understand thoroughly, waxing is not all that cut and dried. Often the snow conditions fall between two waxes. When this happens, *always* try the harder wax first. You can put a softer wax on top of a harder one, but you can't do the opposite. If you need to go from soft to hard, you have to scrape off or blow-torch off the soft and start again from scratch. Soft wax will fight its way out from under a harder wax every time.

The safest way to work up through the waxes is as follows:

1. Put on a thin coat of the hardest wax you think you can use under the conditions. If your skis won't grip well, then:

2. Put on a thicker "kicker" of the same wax. A kicker is a layer of wax covering the center one-third of the ski, the kicking or gripping area. The gliding areas are the tips and tails. If you still slip, then:

3. Either wax the whole ski with the next softest wax or, if you feel you're already pretty close to having it right, just add a kicker of the softer wax.

Be careful, however, not to give up on a wax too soon. Ski on it for about ten minutes before you decide it's not working. It takes wax a while to start doing what it eventually intends to do in terms of gripping.

WORKING WITH APPLICATION: Here's a paradox. Everybody advises you to do your waxing in a nice warm room, putting nice warm wax on nice warm skis. Everybody also advises you never to wax until you arrive where you're going to be skiing, because it's impossible to know how the conditions are going to be until you're at the site. Obviously, then, unless you're skiing in your own backyard, your waxing conditions are usually going to be something less than ideal. For outdoor waxing a blow torch is a great help. But whether you wax in that warm room or outdoors with a blow torch, be sure your skis are dry before you put on wax and be sure to cool them for about ten minutes before you put them flat on the snow or they'll ice/snow up on you.

Doing it the hard way: Hard wax is the easiest to apply. You just scribble it all over the bottoms of the skis as if it were a crayola. Then smooth it out to a fine gloss with a cork, either a real cork or one of the new artificials. Rather than one thick layer, it is better to put on a thin layer, polish it out, let the skis rest and cool for a few minutes, scribble on another layer, polish that one out, etc.

You'll want an extra layer or layers if you're going on a rather long tour and don't want to have to stop and rewax. You'll also need heavier layering if you're on the weighty side. A weightier skier needs more wax than a lighter one. A beginner needs a bit more wax or a slightly softer wax than an experienced skier.

Incidentally, if you're waxing outdoors, don't just peel off the lead foil and drop it. Put it in your pocket and carry it home and throw it away there. Lead is definitely not biodegradable.

Easier than polishing the wax by hand is running over it with a torch or a warm travel iron or one of those special wax irons that are heated with pellets. Easier, yes, but it means you have to have these things with you, and a cork is much lighter and smaller. Anyway, rubbing your

Marc Hardy

The solitude . . .

Ralph Thornton

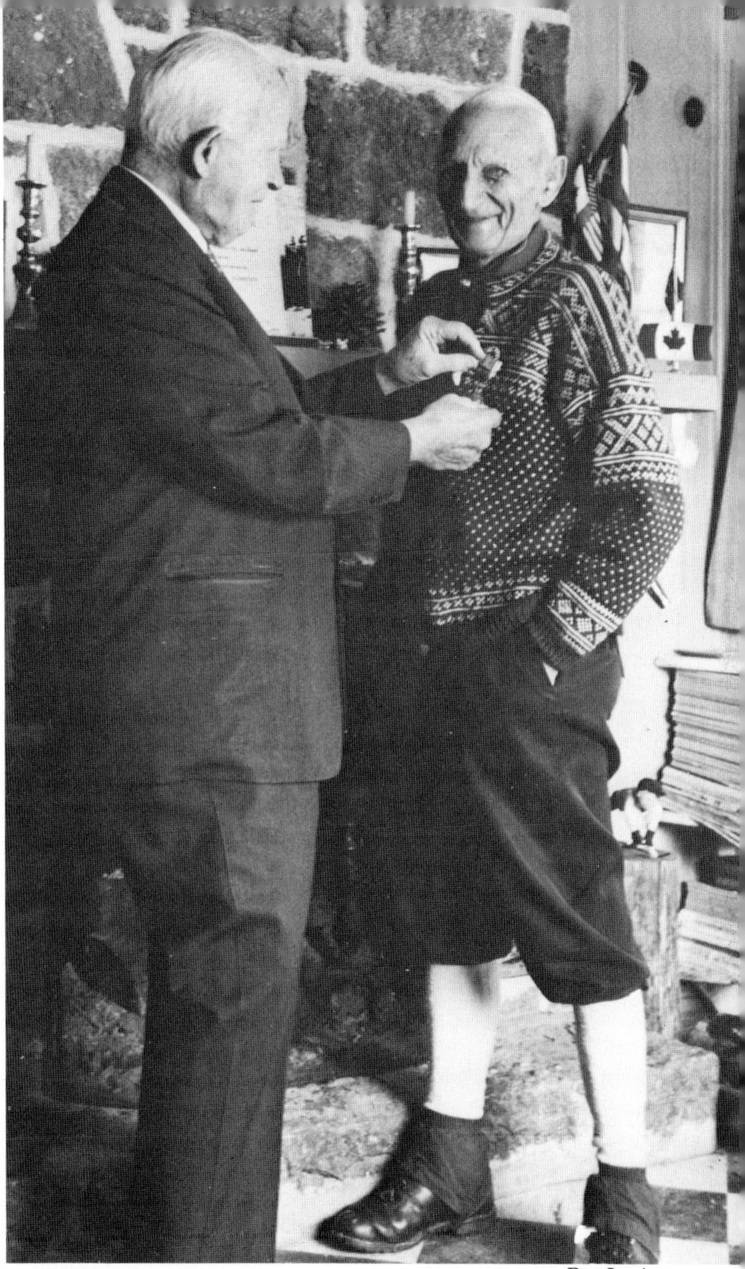

Dan Lewis

Jack Rabbit Johannsen, age 97, having his St. Olaf's Medal admired by Norman Reid, an old 1920's Lake Placid ski buddy.

"Except for the tracks of my skis upon the snow, no one will ever know that I was there."

The groups who go out together stay together and stop and talk together and eat lunch together.

Marc Hardy

Swiss National Tourist Office

Touring skis are recommended only for those whose idea of touring is going off into the nowhere.

The best line up the hill is the one that feels best for you.

Marc Hardy

Marc Hardy

Georges Girard, President of the Mont-Sainte-Anne Ski Club, waxing up.

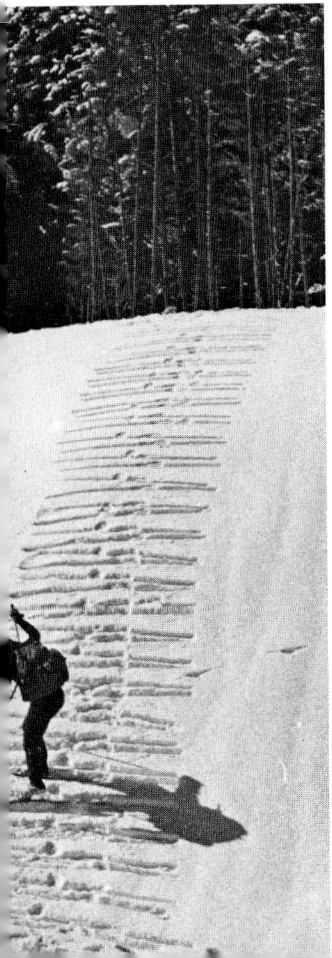

This is what the racers wear.

Swiss National Tourist Office

Marc Hardy

Ski resorts are willing to provide the facilities people seek. Trail grooming and track laying equipment at Laurentides Park, Quebec.

Ralph Thornton

At Scandinavian Lodge all the facilities for learning and enjoying are right outside the door.

Right: Some of the five thousand participants in the twenty-five mile Engadine Ski Marathon, which is run from Maloja to Zuoz, Switzerland, every March.

Swiss National Tourist Office

Barbara Toohey

Ski touring has a universal appeal in Norway. Young marrieds pull their tiny babies in pulkas. *(Below)* Some skiers are almost too young to have the hang of walking yet.

Barbara Toohey

Oslo Travel Association

The Holmenkollen Railway in Oslo, a thirty-minute electric train link to the ski parks.

Marc Hardy

Above: There are oil-stove-heated warming huts at strategic locations in Laurentides Park.

Left: Tote a packful of emergency gear if you are not touring on marked, well-traveled trails.

Marc Hardy

Marc Hardy

"Don't look back. Something may be gaining on you."

skis down with a cork is a good warm-up exercise.

The simplest way of all to wax, especially if you're waxing a whole gang of skis, is to melt the wax in a pot and paint it on with a brush.

You can put hard wax in the grooves, but even better is paraffin or silver downhill wax.

STICKY WICKET: Klister is the messy one. It's double trouble. (At the Trapp Family Lodge it costs twice as much to have klister put on your skis as it does hard wax.) You get it all over yourself and everything within touching distance. At least, I do. An immaculate-looking Scandinavian gentleman in a ski shop once assured me that, "There's nothing to using klister. Just squeeze it on and spread it with one of those little plastic spreaders. You won't get it on yourself or anything else." Perhaps I am by nature a slob, but I *do* get it on my clothes—and everything else. I like the advice given by my one woman instructor, "Get everything out of the way when you use klister. Roll up your sleeves. Make it so you're just hands and klister."

But whether you're a clean klisterer or a chaotic one, the approach is the same. Klister goes on much more easily if it's warm. In fact, some of it won't spread at all unless it's warm. If you're driving to where you're going to be skiing, you could let the klister ride next to the heater outlet or, if you forget to do this, you can warm it on the radiator once you arrive. If you have a torch, make a few passes over the tube with the flame. If you have neither radiator nor torch, stick it inside your clothes next to your hot body until it warms up.

Squeeze the klister onto the ski in a flat ski-trail-like pattern. Start at the tip just after the bend and go down each side of the groove. Do not put klister in the groove and try not to get any on the edges of the skis or it may cause icing/snowing up. Wax the groove with paraffin or silver downhill wax or nothing.

When applying klister, hold the tube so that it's perpendicular to the ski and the whole mouth of the tube is touching the ski. You don't want to hold the tube at, say, a 45° angle, because you'd then be likely to ooze out a fat worm of klister that would be much more than you need. One tube of klister should be enough for three pairs of skis.

Take one of those plastic or metal spreaders and smooth out the klister evenly so that there are no bare spots. You may have to stand back and let the light hit the bottom of the ski in order to see if you've missed any part of it. It helps a great deal in spreading klister if you have a torch to heat the klister and the ski beneath it while you smooth. If you have no torch and the stuff refuses to spread evenly with the spreader, then use the warm heel of your hand. Caution: Don't put your klister-covered hand into your glove or you may wear that item of apparel to your grave. Clean the klister off your hands with mechanic's hand cream or Vaseline.

As with the hard stuff the very easiest way to apply klister is by melting it in a pot and brushing it on.

When you put the klister into your pack or store it away for the summer, be certain you have the lid on tight. There's nothing you can do with a pack that a tube of klister has oozed out into, except throw away the pack and everything in it.

Once you've put klister on your skis and smoothed it out, don't clap the ski bottoms together to carry them off to where you're going to start skiing. That will rough up your smooth surface, and you'll have to do the smoothing job all over again. The best way to carry freshly klistered skis is by the bail of the binding. Caution: Don't step on anything with a klistered ski, unless you want to take that item with you on your tour.

There are now some spray-on klisters in aerosol cans, but they are not yet as effective as the original sticky and are more designed for use on plastic bottoms than on wood. And as one purist instructor put it, "I don't trust anything in aerosol cans."

Base of operations: Most wooden skis have to have their bases treated to keep them from soaking up moisture and to provide a surface to which the wax will stick. Ask your dealer if the ones you buy need this treatment. If they do, most experts agree that the only way to treat them is to burn in a pine tar preparation. There are a lot of easy spray-on and paint-on base preparations available, but they are just not as durable and effective as the old-fashioned, difficult-to-apply kind.

The easiest and safest procedure for burning on pine tar and the one I recommend most heartily is this. Place your skis bottom to bottom and cinch them together with one of those elastic fasteners at top and bottom. Grasp the skis firmly in one hand and in the other clutch a few one-dollar bills. Extend both the hand with the skis and the hand with the dollar bills toward the attendant of a good ski touring-mountaineering shop and request that he pine-tar the bases for you.

If out of virtue or necessity you insist on doing the pine-tarring yourself, the procedure is this. First sand off the protective coat applied by the factory for shipping purposes. Then take your torch and warm the pine tar. Heat the first 18–24 inches of the ski. Paint the warm pine tar onto the heated area of the ski with a brush. Make the layer of pine tar as thin as possible. Keep moving the torch along the painted-on pine tar until you see it separate and start to disappear into the wood. Should the pine tar begin to smoke, you've left the torch on it too long. If you pull the torch away *immediately*, you probably haven't done any permanent damage. When the ski has absorbed all the pine tar it looks as if it's going to, wipe off the rest with a rag. Continue in this manner until you've covered the whole ski.

When you're finished and have wiped off the excess tar, the ski base should be dark brown and dry-feeling, not tacky. If it is tacky, work it over some more with the torch and rag. If, on the other hand, the finished ski base looks white, then it is not finished. You didn't get enough tar on and in, so start the whole process over again.

COMING CLEAN: Cleaning wax off skis is even more of a bore than putting it on. With hard wax you can scrape most of it off with a scraper, then heat what remains with your torch and clean it off with rags. Save every rag you can get your hands on. Ask non-X-C-ing friends to save their rags for you. If you're a fairly active cross-country skier, you'll use up more rags than any one human being or one family can possibly produce. It's like those birth scenes in old movies where the doctor says, "Boil lots of water and bring me all the clean rags you can find." Only you don't need the hot water, and you *do* need as many rags as if quintuplets were being delivered.

With klister the process is the same, only, as always with klister, it's messier.

There are wax removers that you can put on, let rest, then rub off with part of your extensive rag collection. This works beautifully, but it can be expensive, because it takes quite a bit of remover to do the job. Still, if you have a greater supply of money than patience, or if torches scare you, wax remover is a good product to use. It is not to be used, however, on plastic-bottomed skis unless the instructions clearly state that it can be.

LESS IS MORE: Everyone usually ends the season with klister on his skis, since klister is what's used for spring snow. There are two theories on what you should do about storing your klistered skis. One theory is that you should clean them to a state of pristine immaculosity and then put them away. The other theory—and it's the one I follow—is that a nice coating of klister protects the skis over the summer. Also, I find that you feel more like cleaning them in the fall when you're full of the adrenalin of anticipation for the season ahead.

An interesting sidelight to storing the skis with klister is what the old X-C master, Sven Wiik, once did. His wife, Birthe, stored her skis with the klister on them. Then when winter arrived and the mountains around Steamboat Springs filled up with their highly touted "champagne powder," the Wiiks decided to go on their first ski tour. They gathered with a few touring friends to wax before taking off. Birthe started to clean off the klister. "Oh, just leave it on and ski on it," said Sven casually. Amazed, his friends looked up from their business of scribbling on the special green. "Klister on fresh powder?" They began to get the idea that Sven was planning to dispose of his good wife in the wilderness by miring her forever into the snow. But trusting Birthe did as Sven advised, and, lo, she had the best wax of anybody on the tour. Over the summer the klister had dried out and become harder than the hardest hard wax.

Another Wiik variation in dry powder is to ski on the pine tar without any running wax at all. But the ability to know when to leave well enough alone in waxing doesn't come overnight. As Sven explains it, "It took me ten years to learn how to *not* wax skis."

A MISTAKE IS AS GOOD AS A MILE: This waxing chapter is really just a once-over-lightly. You must, as the progressive educators say, "learn by doing." You must, also, unfortunately, learn by making mistakes. If it's any comfort, experts make waxing mistakes too. Every day. Many is the racer who has had to drop out because he waxed wrong and there was no time to stop and wax right. And in Klosters I saw my instructor, who was an Olympic alternate, giving a private lesson to a countess, and both of them were cemented to the track, because he'd used the wrong-color klister.

Sometimes you start out with the correct wax and the conditions change in the middle of the tour. Suddenly you're waxed wrong. Then you can rewax and ski a while and find the wax is wrong again. Sometimes the wax is right when you're on the track and wrong when you get off in the powder. Sometimes it's right in the sun and wrong when you hit the shady patches. This is just a part of what makes waxing such a challenge. (Challenge = something you can hardly cope with.)

Still, there is one beautiful thing about wax. You can lay the blame for all your skiing problems on it. If there's ever a day when you simply can't get it together—you're off your stride and you can't climb a molehill—you can always mutter, "It's that #@!!??* wax."

WAXING ENTHUSIASTIC: But waxing has its truly good side, too. Sometimes, if the snow conditions don't change, you can use the same wax day after day after day after day. And when wax is right, it's really right. Nothing can match a well-waxed ski for that ecstatic winged-foot feeling. Such ecstacy is well worth the sometime agony of the waxing process. This is why most of us remain waxophiles in spite of ourselves.

5. DRESSING FOR IT

I THINK I'm going to get myself into serious trouble now. I'm going to knock something that will bring the wrath of the nation upon me. It's that hallowed youth-cult raiment, that honest garment of honest labor, that attire that won the West, blue jeans or, as they are called in California, Levi's.

For cross-country skiing, next to a suit of armor or a deep-sea diver's outfit, jeans are the worst selection you can make. The legs are usually too skinny for free knee movement. Denim is the least waterproof of fabrics. It drinks in water like Pat Boone drinks in milk, and it holds that water until it freezes and stiffens so that you feel as if you're skiing in cold cardboard. Jeans give less than no protection from the cold. You would literally be better off skiing in your long underwear.

The reason I rant on against blue jeans for ski touring is that I've seen so many blue—both in skin color and in the emotional sense of the word—X-C skiers wearing them. It's not the skiers' fault, either. It's the fault of the X-C books and articles and brochures that, in citing the inexpensive joys of the sport, burble, "You don't need fancy clothes. Just jump into an old pair of jeans, snap on your skis, and have a ball!"

True, you don't need fancy clothes, but you *do* need comfortable clothes that you can move easily in and that will keep you warm and dry. That is just what jeans are not. In case I haven't made myself clear, I don't think much of jeans for ski touring, and I would suggest you avoid them.

While I'm being negative and profligate, I'd like also to come out against wearing your old downhill ski pants for X-C. Even if they're all stretched out, they're still not all *that* stretched out, and with every step you take the stirrups engage in a tug of war with your knees. With this handicap you can tire yourself out twice as fast as normal.

COLD COMFORT: The basic idea of cross-country clothing is comfort. You want neither to become as overheated as a boiled sausage nor as core-cold as a popsicle. Obviously, unless you're skiing in an electric suit with a temperature control, you're not going to get this comfort out of one item of clothng. You must, as the musicians put it, "take five" so that you can regulate yourself like a thermostat by adding or subtracting layers of clothing as your temperature requires. Here are the basic five:

1. Underwear
2. Turtleneck
3. Shirt
4. Sweater
5. Windbreaker

Down below the layering doesn't need to be quite as extensive. Underwear, socks, and pants should do it, unless you are unusually cold-natured or the weather is unusually cold, in which case add a pair of warm-up pants.

On a really cold morning you set off with everything on and ski for five or ten minutes or until you feel your own central heating system start to function, but *before* you start to sweat. Then take off whatever you feel is excessive and stuff it into your pack or tie it around your waist. Perhaps you'll take off the sweater but leave on the windbreaker. Perhaps you'll take off both. Whenever you stop for lunch or an extended rest, put most of everything back on to avoid getting chilled. All day you'll be adding or shedding, or you should be, if you want the comfort that along with ease is the goal of ski touring.

Naturally, if you're doing spring skiing and you know it's not going to get bitterly cold, you can eliminate some of the layers before taking off. But just to be on the safe side, you may want to carry them along, if you're going a long way from home or lodge or car.

SKIER IN SHEEP'S CLOTHING: Pulling the wool over your eyes—and down over your body—is the best thing to do for X-C skiing comfort. Wool is warmer than any other fabric. It's even warm when it's wet. This is because it doesn't conduct heat away from the body, and when next to the skin it dries out from body heat.

Cotton, on the other hand, stays wet and keeps you cold. Dacron is better than cotton but tends to trap in moisture and gives you a clammy feeling.

BENEATH IT ALL: It's particularly important to have wool next to your skin where warmth is most important. Consequently, wool underwear is the best kind, unless you're allergic to it. The itch of wool is a problem, but it's something most of us can get used to for its other advantages. If you're excessively sensitive to itching, you could invest—and invest is the right word for it—in cashmere underwear. Another possibility to get cashmere with less cash is to haunt Good Will stores and rummage sales (especially those held in the more exclusive areas of town) to see if you can find some old tattered and torn cashmere sweaters to wear underneath your turtleneck.

There are also some effective combinations with wool, such as the supersoft Viyella. This is 55 percent lambswool and 45 percent cotton. The thermal underwear of downhill skiing fame is 40 percent wool, 50 percent cotton, and 10 percent nylon. Both of these have a thin layer of cotton next to the skin, enough to cut down on the itch factor, but hopefully not enough to induce the soggy factor.

If you're so sensitive to wool that you can't stand it even in combination, then you could go for orlon or a version of fishnet that contains no wool. Fishnet underwear is highly touted for X-C use. It is designed to trap the heat and yet let the moisture evaporate. It comes in all cotton, half and half cotton and polyester, and in a cotton and wool combination. Not surprisingly, the last version is considered best and the greater the percentage of wool the better. The only trouble is that it's almost impossible to find. The only place I've ever seen it was on the leg of the instructor of my survival class, when he peeled down his knee socks to show it to us.

TURTLENECKS, SHIRTS, AND SWEATERS: Your second, third, and fourth layers are pretty flexible. A turtleneck is a turtleneck is a turtleneck. The shirt can be any kind of light wool you happen to have around or if you're wearing one of the Scandinavian X-C knit suits, the shirt from that.

The sweater should be wool and loosely knit so that it can breathe easily. It should also fit loosely so that you can breathe easily. Those Irish and Icelandic and Eskimo varieties that have a lot of lanolin left in are especially warm.

WINDBREAKERS: Here's another flexible one. Any old windbreaker will do, but the lighter weight and the more water-repellent the better. The Scandinavian poplin kind that matches the knickers makes a trim-looking outfit. The down parkas that are such favorites with downhill skiers are not generally advised for touring. They're likely to be too hot when you're chugging along. I've seen them used, and I've used one myself in really cold weather, and I confess I was glad to have it on. Here's another case of just try to find what works for you personally and wear that. Cross-country clothing rules are made to be bent all out of shape.

KNICKERS: There's another mystique to ski touring besides waxing. It's an anti-style mystique. To most cross-country skiers in this country the very idea of high-style attire is abhorrent. Chic makes them sick. Probably it's a reaction to the excessive-going-on-phony style-consciousness of downhillers. But whyever, most American X-C-ers go out of their way to avoid looking stylish.

It's a pity, therefore, that knickers and knee socks have become stylish in downhill circles and that they look so good, thereby making a necessity seem a foppery. And knickers and knee socks are a virtual necessity. Only knickers give that good loose-knee-joint freedom you require for the sport. Only the close-to-the-leg fit of the knee socks keeps the clothing tangle away from the ankles and keeps you from having soggy or snow-logged cuffs. To see what I mean try X-C-ing in flare bottoms sometime.

You can keep some of the taint of style out of your knickers and knee socks by buying old wool pants at the Good Will or at any army surplus store and converting them to knickers at home, being sure not to do such a good job on the conversion that they belie their humble origins. You can also get knee socks that are moth-eaten and not quite long enough to meet the knickers. You may get a little chilled where the gap is, but like the women who suffered to be stylish in thin heels and pointed toes a few years back, you sometimes have to suffer to be non-stylish.

If, however, you're willing to wear comfortable and functional clothing even if it happens to look as if you're style-conscious and dressing for effect, then, here are some choices in the store-bought knicker line.

1. Poplin: this is a strong, tightly woven, finely corded fabric. The kind used in knickers is either all cotton or a cotton and dacron combination. It sometimes goes under fancy names like "Raymar." The best of the poplin knickers are made in the Scandinavian countries, although we're beginning to catch on to how it's done.

Poplin knickers are fairly water-repellent and quite durable, especially those in the dacron-cotton combination. They are good both in cold weather and for spring skiing. Some lace below the knees; others are fastened with Velcro closers. I noticed that every Norwegian instructor at Yosemite Ski School was wearing poplin knickers and I don't think it was just chauvinism in action.

2. Stretch or Crepe Nylon: This is what the racers wear. The knickers are almost always bought as suits with a shirt or jacket of the same knit material. Usually it's a 60 percent mixture with cotton. Red and blue with white piping are the popular colors, although other colors and white tops are also available. Since these aren't as warm

and wind-resistant as the harder surfaced fabrics, most skiers prefer to use them only for racing or at least flat-track skiing when their internal heating system is going full blast or for spring skiing in klister weather when the external heating system begins to warm up.

These suits are very good-looking and as their popularity increases, so do their prices. Before long it will probably reach the point that you can fly to Scandinavia to buy your X-C attire and save enough to pay for the flight, rather like going overseas to buy a car in the old days.

3. Nylon: These knickers come in hard-surface, wind- and water-repellent nylon fabric like the kind of material used in windbreakers. Some are single-layer, some double-layer. Most fasten with Velcro. These are especially good for cold-weather skiing.

4. Any Fabric at All: If you can't find any of the above, knickers in virtually any fabric, except maybe dotted swiss, will be usable. Corduroy has the disadvantage of being a water drinker, but the advantage of being readily obtainable in mountaineering and hiking and hunting shops.

A good kind of knickers that I've mostly seen only in the shops of the Alpine countries are those made of the same kind of stretch fabric as downhill ski pants. These allow you to move easily, yet they keep you warm and dry. Very good for cold-weather skiing.

And there's always good old wool, which many hardy X-C-ers, including my survival instructor, consider the best choice of all.

Warm-up pants: If you do a lot of cold-weather skiing, you should have a pair of warm-up pants to pull on over your knickers when the temperature is especially low or you stop and don't want to cool off too fast. These can be either the shiny, windbreaker, water-repellent material of downhill "powder pants" or the knit nylon variety that are like those worn as warm-up pants in track and basketball. These last can be matched up with the stretch nylon racing outfits, making a suit with two pairs of pants. If the weather is wet and cold, the hard-surface kind work better.

Some skiers—even one instructor I had—actually prefer to ski in the knit warm-up pants instead of knickers, claiming them to be more comfortable. (The instructor's girl friend maintained that he wore them because he considered his legs too skinny to look good in knickers.)

Hats: A knit hat is best, because it's easy to carry in your pack or parka pocket, and it can be worn down over your ears or not, as the temperature requires. The most versatile variety of the knit hat is the Balaclava, which rolls down into a semi-face mask for really cold weather.

A knit headband is also handy. It keeps your ears warm when you don't need a hat and it augments their warmth on days that you do.

Never underestimate the value of a hat in body heat regulation. You lose up to 60 percent of your body heat from your head. There's another old but true cold-weather cliche: If your feet are cold, put on your hat.

Conversely, when you're heated up, snapping off your hat can be the fastest cooler-offer.

SOCKS: For socks, again wool is the best choice. Avoid cotton. When I was using my old one-size-too-large boots, I wore cotton tennis socks to try to make the boots fit. As a result my feet were so swampy that I almost expected alligators to emerge when I took off the boots.

There are also some wool and synthetic combinations that are not too bad, and others in all acrylic that are not too good.

MITTENS AND GLOVES: At the risk of sounding like a hireling of the sheepherders' union, I have to say it's wool again and for the same old reason of wet warmth. A little nylon for strength and shape-keeping, as in the Norwegian Ragg mittens, is okay. A good combination for all conditions is a pair of wool mittens with a waterproof shell of nylon duck that you can pull on in wet weather.

If you go for leather gloves or mittens, be sure the leather is something like deer or buckskin or antelope. The most-often-used leather for downhill gloves and mittens, horsehide, turns totally stiff if you get it wet. I used an old pair of downhill gloves when I took a survival course in the rain and when the gloves dried out the next day, they were like bronze castings of themselves.

The ongoing mitten versus gloves controversy winds up a matter of taste and temperature. Mittens are warmer; gloves give you more feel in your poling.

For those who enjoy spending money there are special ski touring gloves with leather palms and fingertips and a mesh top for ventilation. And I saw a pair of driving gloves being worn by a California highway patrolman who was giving me a ticket that looked as if they'd be ideal for X-C.

THE LITTLE THINGS THAT COUNT:

1. Spats and Gaiters: These are invaluable when you're going through deep, fresh snow, since with their elastic cuffs and strap under the foot they keep your boots from filling up. They come in three levels: the spats that just go up to the ankle, the midcalf short gaiters, and the long ones that reach clear to the knee.

2. Rubber Boot Covers: When you're sloshing through the slush in klister weather, rubber boot covers can keep your boots and socks from sponging up the wet. Usually they are a bright blue color. You just tug them on over your boots and clamp yourself into the bindings as usual.

3. Boot Socks: You can buy wool boot covers to keep your feet warm during the coldest tours, but why buy, when an old pair of socks with the toes cut out will work just as well?

4. Poncho: If you ski in an area where the rains come, a folding-into-itself waterproof poncho can be the most useful item in your pack. There are few worse things than being several miles from home with the rain soaking through every one of your five layers.

SUPERCHIC: Yes, Virginia and Virgil, there is a movement toward really stylish and really expensive touring suits. The movement, of course, is coming mainly from American ski clothing manufacturers, who are twitching visibly at the thought of a great new virtually untapped market. Now, if you put your mind to it, you can pay $80–$100 for a little touring ensemble. But beware if you do. There's a lot of reverse snobbery in X-C. If you show up looking like something out of *Vogue* or *Gentleman's Quarterly*, your fine feathers may get you the ugly duckling treatment.

6. WHERE TO DO IT

ONE OF THE advantages frequently cited for ski touring is that you can do it wherever there's snow —right out your back or front door, down the road, through Central Park, across a golf course. Anywhere. You don't have to go to ski resorts and can, therefore, save piles of money by being able to avoid their bloated prices. True.

It's equally true, however, that some of the best ski touring facilities are in resorts. It's only logical. Ski resorts are located in areas where the snow is good. They are set up to handle snow sports. They want people to come and spend and so they are willing to provide the facilities people seek, such as, in the case of ski touring, instruction, prepared tracks, and marked trails. And as you will learn in the survival chapter, these facilities are not just frills. They are necessities for those of us who aren't Sherpa-blooded Eagle Scouts.

Most of the major ski resorts are now developing cross-country programs. Especially well established and highly recommended is Steve Rieschl's school at Vail. The Aspen complex is blessed with two touring setups: Ashcroft and Chuck Fothergill's. Jackson Hole with all that flatland and all those photogenic mooses is another good bet with two. Sun Valley is developing fast in ski touring. In Sugarbush, X-C is sneaking up rapidly on downhill. Each season the list grows. Check the Appendix and you're sure to find areas with ski touring facilities that appeal to you.

Besides the resorts that have cross-country skiing as a sideline, there are a few—very few, but we can hope for more—real cross-country centers. In these ski touring is the big thing, the main event, the spotlighted attraction. Here you can find the total X-C experience. And if you're looking for the compleat ski touring ecstatic, memorable vacation, a few of these few are long-established five-star winners in the vital categories of: Instruction; Tracks and Trails and Tours; Scenery; Accommodations and Cuisine; Ambiance, a French word meaning all kinds of things like atmosphere, good vibes, and, to ring in another foreign word, *Gemütlichkeit.*

YOSEMITE NATIONAL PARK

Yosemite, California

Instruction: Here the cross-country school is under the aegis of the Mountaineering School, which is directed by the aptly named Wayne Merry. Merry runs one of the happiest ski school ships in the country. Ski instructors, who are notorious grumblers over their working conditions, have nothing but praise for Merry's direction, and their contentment is reflected in their teaching and transmitted to their students. The school is run strictly on the merit system as witnessed by the fact that Merry chose a woman, Norwegian, University of California graduate, Trine Bech, to head up the X-C school, "because she is the best."

Yosemite has probably the greatest range of instruction of any touring center in this country. Their lesson program includes: basic classes, intermediate classes, advanced classes, private instruction, racing coaching, children's classes, touring survival, special ski camping, snow camping, one-day tours, overnight tours, special trips for *very* advanced skiers. To support this teaching program there is a complete rental, repair, and sales shop.

Each year in March the X-C school puts on a Nordic Weekend that includes a 10-kilometer (7-mile) touring race. This is one of those for-everybody races. Last year the ages of the participants ranged from eight to seventy-five. The main purpose of this kind of race is just to finish the course at your own speed, rather than to strain out a new record. This is the kind of noncompetitive competition that is ideal for us for-the-fun-of-it types.

Tracks and Trails and Tours: Since the X-C instruction is usually given up in the high meadows of Yosemite rather than down on the valley floor, there is no official track. The classes usually stomp out their own when they arrive at the scene. It makes a good warm-up exercise.

Throughout the park numerous trails are mapped out for you in the Yosemite winter brochure. And when the snow is good you can skim around sightseeing in the valley. The best idea, though, is to sign up for one of the scheduled tours or, if you have your own group, to book a tour leader. Much of Yosemite is wilderness, and it's a bad idea for an X-C tenderfoot to drift around the wilderness on his own, unless he has a taste for frostbite and hypothermia.

Scenery: What can you say about a touring center located in what is one of the scenic wonder areas of the world? And it's Yosemite in *winter*, which means private Yosemite, free from the people-polluting hordes of summer. The beauties of winter in Yosemite are something special in themselves. In the clear, cold air Yosemite shines as it must have for its original Indian residents, with the crystallized falls scattering down the gray granite walls into giant ice punch bowls, the trees woolly with snow, and the ice wrinkling the still ponds.

The fact that the touring takes place in such spectacular surroundings is enough to take anyone's X-C bug and incubate it into a raging fever for the sport.

Accommodations and Cuisine: The accommodations range from the relatively spartan Camp Curry with its oil-stove-heated cabins to the totally modern and attractive motel-like facilities of Yosemite Lodge to the sybaritic opulence of the Ahwahnee. This last deserves special mention as a *sui generis* spectacular among the world's great hotels.

Immediately upon entering the Ahwahnee you have a

feeling of infinite space. Everything is on a huge scale with fireplaces large enough to roast Paul Bunyan's blue ox and great halls in which you could install a modern three-story, six-unit apartment and still have room for a tennis court and swimming pool. They don't build 'em like that any more. The Ahwahnee was constructed back in the late twenties and reflects the optimistic opulence of the times. All is done in an Indian motif with artifacts for art and Indian signs everywhere you look, including along the beams of the ceilings. The bedrooms have every modern comfort and every stunning view of the valley.

Dining takes place in yet another great hall, which, with its high-beamed ceilings and candlelight flickering off two-story windows, resembles a rustic Versailles. It's hard to be objective about the quality of the food when you're as whelmed as you are by the surroundings and as starved as you are from the exercise, but I have always thought of it as excellent. There are many choices and many courses and the chef is particularly talented in his sauce-making and dessert creation. Even should you stay in lesser digs than the Ahwahnee, you owe it to your memory bank to have at least one dinner in the Ahwahnee dining room, although the cafeteria and the Mountain Room Broiler at the Yosemite Lodge have much to recommend them. The Mountain Room has, along with its commendable selection of steaks and chops, spectacular mountain photography lining the walls and even more spectacular views from the floor-to-ceiling windows.

Ambiance: Yosemite, itself, is the star, but the park's animals make a great supporting cast. By morning there are the coyotes that you see out on their breakfast excursions performing ritual mouse dances on the snow. By night there are the panhandling raccoons staring at you through their masked eyes, brazenly demanding forbidden handouts with the success of their season of begging bulging around their fat middles.

The human animals, both in residence and visiting, are of the extremely pleasant and relaxed variety. You can get to know them at the twice-weekly ski buffets, at the Ahwahnee's second-floor replica of an old gold mine town, the El Dorado Diggins, at one of the ski or nature films and lectures, and dancing at the Ahwahnee's Indian Room.

In Yosemite Valley you feel you are in splendid isolation, totally away from it all—meaning all the bad things the world is trying to ram down your throat—and you never want to leave.

SCANDINAVIAN LODGE AND MT. WERNER TRAINING CENTER
Steamboat Springs, Colorado

Instruction: For a cross-country skier, going to Steamboat Springs is like going to Tibet if you're a transcendental meditator, because at Steamboat dwells the guru of cross-country, Sven Wiik. Not that he's old in years, it's just in experience and knowledge that he's venerable. A partial list of his past service to skiing includes Chairman of the Organizing Committee of the North American Nordic Ski Championships, President of the U.S. Ski Association, Director of the USSA National Coaches School, Head Coach of the U. S. FIS Cross-country and Nordic Combined Ski Team, the U. S. University Nordic Team, and the U. S. Olympic Cross-Country and Nordic Combined ski team. Whew! and Double Whew! On top of that, practically every director of every ski touring school in this country has studied with Sven at one time or other in one of his ski clinics at the Mt. Werner Training Center.

You might think that someone who trains champion racers and is Swedish (a national group with a reputation for demanding a lot of their bodies) might run a tough, whack 'em in the shins and run 'em ragged ski school. Not so. Sven is a gentle and patient man and it comes through in the methods of his instructors. You learn a lot without realizing it and seemingly without effort.

You can also learn a certain amount by osmosis. There are usually a few Olympic hopefuls in residence, and once a week there's an all-comers-welcome night race. (The racers wear lights similar to miner's lamps on their heads.)

If X-C isn't enough exercise for you, there is a gym in which you can work out. If X-C is too much for you, there's a sauna in which you can unwind.

There is also a rental shop and a sales shop that can meet your every touring need, some of which you probably didn't even know you had.

Tracks and Trails and Tours: All the facilities for learning and enjoying are right on the spot out the door of the lodge. There's a track, which in summer doubles as a soccer field. There's a short race course cleverly designed to give you practice in every kind of technique. (Of course, it *should* be cleverly designed, since track and trail drawing is another area of Sven's expertise. A Wiik race course is on a par with a Robert Trent Jones golf course.) There's also a marked trail up and around and through the woods across the road from the lodge.

For day or half-day tours you should drive up to Rabbit Ears Pass and make tracks of your own led by one of the Wiik family or their disciples. This is the essence of cross-country across rolling acres of undemanding terrain through woods of moss-hung trees, making you feel as if you're the first—or the last—inhabitants of the earth.

In spring there's an added treat, ski-touring fishing excursions with the chef, Evert Forneman.

Scenery: Out your room's window from the deck of the lodge or as you pause to gulp oxygen on the race course, everywhere you look is Colorado, and looking at it you understand the Denver *Post* saying, " 'Tis a privilege to live in Colorado."

Mt. Werner's imposing presence looks benignly down on a wide-open sunny valley full of bare aspens and snow-dressed firs and pines and over all the translucent blue bowl of sky. If that's not enough to keep your eyes off your ski tips, then nothing is.

Accommodations and Cuisine: Nowhere are accommodations more accommodating. Everything is new and done in Danish modern, that appealing decor that both modernists and traditionalists can live with compatibly. Birthe Wiik, Sven's wife, is Danish and has the magic decorating touch for which her countrymen and women are noted. And she doesn't just leave more than well enough alone. She keeps changing a painting here, a ceramic bowl there, a weaving somewhere else, so that as guests return time after time—as Scandinavian Lodge guests are wont to do—they always find something different to delight in, making the lodge seem like a living, changing entity.

Besides the thirty super-comfortable rooms, there are a few nearby cabins available for rent.

The food is gloriously Scandinavian. Every time they ring the dinner bell you find yourself reacting like Pavlov's dog in anticipation. In the morning the breakfast table is already set with freshly squeezed orange juice and homemade apple sauce and marmalade served in ceramic bowls made by Birthe Wiik and Christine Forneman, the chef's wife. They also have handwoven the place mats. Breakfast sets the tone for the rest of the day's meals. Everything is scrupulously fresh and meticulously prepared and handcrafted by talented hands.

The meals are served smörgasbord style. You help yourself and take all you want, but you're supposed to eat all you take. Someone who has lived through the deprivations of wartime Denmark, as did Birthe, does not go along with the idea of leaving a bit of polite waste on the plate. But why are we talking about leaving food? Who would leave a trace of Evert Forneman's home-marinated herring or pea soup with a dollop of mustard or potato pancakes as light as the Steamboat powder or cod with creamy egg sauce or Swedish pancakes with snowberries or homemade bread or *anything?*

As you sit down to your meal, you offer up thanks that you're pursuing a wonderfully calorie-burning sport like X-C so you can eat to your taste buds' content without fear.

Ambiance: "We get the kind of people who need a vacation and want special care and personal attention. That's why our atmosphere is homey." That's Birthe talking, and it is she who is the main generator of this atmosphere in the Scandinavian Lodge. And homey it is. Without its being oppressive, you feel you are a part of a very warm family. You participate in holiday observances like Christmas tree trimming and the dawn Swedish Santa Lucia ceremony on December 13, when the daughter of the house, Birgitta, wears the traditional candles in her hair. Birgitta is such an unspoiled and engaging teenager that it makes you feel there's hope for the world after all. Since the Wiiks have such a good specimen of the art of child-raising themselves, they have a receptive attitude toward all children and young people. They are welcome here as they are at few ski lodges in the country.

Another distinction of the Scandinavian Lodge is the unbooze factor. There is no bar and nothing alcoholic is served with meals. Not that the Wiiks are bluenosed teetotalers; they like a cocktail or a glass of wine as much as anyone. It's just that they don't want to attract the loud and sometimes bellicose drinking crowd. You can, of course, bring your own bottle and have a snort or so in your room, but more likely you'll discover you develop a "who needs it?" attitude and find yourself settling comfortably into a nondrinking pattern.

The final homey touch is provided by Sarek, the Fornemans' Labrador and the two house cats, Charlie and his (probably) daughter.

All in all, you can well understand the group of skiing doctors and their wives from Minnesota who tried a different resort every year seeking perfection. When they hit the Scandinavian Lodge the quest was over. They've been back every December.

FAR HILLS INN
Val Morin, Québec, Canada

Instruction: Are you ready for a Polish ski instructor? No joke. The head of the Far Hills Inn X-C School, Albert Pomian, was born in Poland's High Tatras, and if he wasn't born on the boards, he has been on them regularly since age four. The credentials of this Banacek of the Laurentians further include Alpine racing championships, mountaineer guiding and several years of assisting Lars Larsen in his Aspen cross-country program. Pomian's school has a staff of five of which at least two are always on duty.

The basic strides are taught on the flat of the tennis court—without the net. The first descents and turns are made on a little hill out back below the dining room view window. Then it's off onto the trail for the practical completion of the two-hour lesson, which transforms you from a beginner into an intermediate.

The Far Hills X-C School has a program with a heart

as well as muscle structure. Betty Lucas, wife of the man in command of the Inn's operation, discovered that there were some local school children who, despite the fact that they were growing up in the snowy north countree, had never been on skis. For many of them money was the big obstacle. Betty Lucas, mother of three, inaugurated a program of free instruction and free use of the equipment for these neighborhood children.

And speaking of equipment, you need never worry about renting a set of sick skis or battered boots at the Far Hills Inn. All the skis and boots are sold off at the end of each season and replaced with new for the next.

At the Inn you can hire an instructor to lead you on a tour, but why bother? For one Canadian dollar you can buy the most complete and readable trail map available in any North American ski center and be your own guide.

Tracks and Trails and Tours: Quote from a snowed observer of the Far Hills Inn trail network: "This is what I thought all X-C trails would be like, but now I realize these are just the ideal." The reason the fifty-two-mile network of twenty-two trails *is* ideal is a ninety-seven-year-old reason. It's Jack Rabbit Johannsen. Most of the Far Hills Inn trails are portions of the famous Maple Leaf trail which he laid out in the 1930's.

A few years ago the Lucases looked at the land around the Inn and were suddenly struck by the realization that it was perfect terrain for ski touring. Refreshing approach, that. Often resorts decide that X-C is the new fad and money-maker and, despite totally inappropriate terrain, declare themselves a touring paradise. When the

Lucases hired a trail-making team, it didn't take the team long to discover the job had already been done. It was just a matter of clearing away the thirty to forty years of growth from Jack Rabbit's handiwork. As one of the team put it, "The man's a genius. He's used every ripple of the land to the best advantage."

So there they are waiting for you. Clearly marked with ribbons and signs. Clearly indicated on the map. Clearly as close to perfection as you can find in cross-country trails. All right outside the door of the Inn.

Scenery: One of the reasons for the perfection of the trails is evident when you look over the scene and scenery. It's the *ski de promenade* classic rolling woodsy terrain. Rolling to give you the desired one-third up, one-third down, and one-third flat and woodsy to protect you from the blasted wintry blasts.

The woods also provide a good measure of scenic beauty. The tunnels through the trees recall the country lanes of the provinces of France. The curly barked birches look as if someone had worked them over with a plane and left the curled shavings hanging. The giant evergreens all look as if they're auditioning to be the White House Christmas tree. The trails also pass by and over a whole gang of lakes or *lacs,* as they're spelled in these French parts. In the spring when the snow starts to melt and uncovers the ice, they shine as if silver-plated.

The trails are arranged to give you a number of *vues panoramiques.* From these lookout points you can gaze across the Laurentians, the world's oldest mountains, with their peaks filed down by time into rounded domes.

Accommodations and Cuisine: The Far Hills Inn was once a star of the Laurentian's galaxy of all-season resort hotels. Then it entered into a decline. Now, however, it is restored to its former eminence, and then some. This is due to the able direction of Ted Lucas. No, able is too weak a word for a master hotelier, who at the age of twenty-one was already running a French hotel and just prior to coming to Far Hills spent seven years directing a resort in the Bahamas. With the unofficial but obviously tireless and enthusiastic assistance of his wife, the Far Hills Inn fairly glows from the care it's receiving.

As soon as the Inn started on its new upward course, talent began coming in out of the Canadian wilderness. Now they have Belgian pianiste-chanteur Gerry Soetermans entertaining in the Bar Panoramique when night covers the view. Now they also have a Swiss-French chef, who makes modified American plan unmodified delight for the guests. Every dinner has four choices of main dish. And it's some hour of decision, when you have to select between *Le Canard du Lac de Brome Bigarade* and *Le Roti de Porc Sauce Diable* and *Le Foie de Veau à la Suisse* and *Les Queues de Langoustines Grillés* (like mini-lobster tails covered with delicately and deliciously seasoned crumbs and broiled to orange-gold brown).

The main course does not stand alone. Sometimes you begin with a *quiche Lorraine* and sometimes a *pâté maison* that brings down the house. And always there's French bread that *is* French bread—great round peasant chunks of it with a chewy-crisp crust lightly dusted with flour. This is made by another of the Lucases' local discoveries, a baker who also turns out the resolution-shattering pastries and gateaux that are on every dinner menu and usually on every guest's dessert plate.

Every Saturday night all *enfer* breaks loose with a gigantic buffet featuring wall to wall food, including just by way of example, fresh crab and lobster. After one of these cuisine-o-ramas the guests have been known to literally stand up and cheer the chef, although no one in the room would be able to deal with an encore.

Ambiance: Here is ambiance that knows the meaning of the word. Heavily French it is or, rather, lightly French, since things French tend to be airy instead of leaden. As in all of the province of Quebec, most of the staff is French-speaking. But it is also English-speaking. (Canada's goal is for everybody to be bilingual.) Even the Far Hills Inn's architecture is Anglo-French with its gray French stone first story and its English-looking white wood upper. All the signs, brochures, menus and even the trail map (*pistes de ski de fond*) are in both languages.

In actuality a trip to this section of French Canada is like a trip to France without the passport, without the agonies of a transoceanic flight, without the expense, and, as one Québecker put it, "without the smell."

Besides being French in atmosphere, the Far Hills Inn is also relaxed in its tempo. There is no you've-got-to-be-doing-something-every-minute social director frenzy. You're left alone to do whatever you want—tour the trails at your own speed, swim in the indoor pool (*défense de plonger*), sweat it out in the sauna, or just sit in the bar in your stocking feet sipping a red-eye (a Northwest territory quencher composed of tomato juice and beer) and staring into the fire, letting your atavistic instincts well up, and maybe scratching the skull of Jake, the house dog, 185 pounds of black fur-covered Newfoundland love.

The Far Hills Inn motto is "*Si facile à aimer, si difficile à quiter*" ("So easy to love, so hard to leave"). And since it's also so easy to get to—only a half hour from Montreal over a freeway—it's perfectly understandable that pleasure-loving North American X-C-er's are beating a new trail to its door.

TRAPP FAMILY LODGE
Stowe, Vermont

Instruction: Under the guidance of Johannes von Trapp, the youngest member of the famous singing family, the teaching here has become that most rare thing in X-C, well-organized lessons with all instructors teaching the same techniques. In this period of burgeoning interest in cross-country many places will take anyone with a Norwegian accent and a pair of knickers and turn him loose to do whatever he wants with his classes. Not so at the Trapp Family Lodge, which pioneered X-C in this country way back in the year 1968.

The head of the school is Larry Damon, who was on four—count them—four Olympic teams. His wife, Babben, also teaches and well she should. Gliding under her maiden name of Enger, she took a gold medal back to Norway from the Grenoble Olympics. To give you an idea of the scope of this school, there are a total of fifteen instructors, eight of whom are on duty at any given time.

Two other things are different about the teaching at the Trapps'. The lessons are only one hour long. It is Johannes' theory that, unlike Alpine skiing where you do a lot of standing around and lift riding, in X-C you're at it every minute, and sixty of such minutes are enough to wear out the average novice.

The other difference in the lessons is that you get out on the trail immediately. Johannes maintains that people don't like the walking-a-treadmill sensation of going round and round a track to learn technique. Therefore, in the beginning lesson you really ski, along one of the flatter trails like Sugar Road.

For skiers who already have a modicum of technique there are two-hour guided tours combined with instruction and all-day guided picnic trips which make the three and a half mile run up to Slayton Pasture cabin.

The ski rental shop is another well thought out operation. Even on the most crowded weekend—and some weekends seven to eight hundred people ski here—you get onto your freshly waxed skis in less time than it takes a short-order cook to turn out a fried egg. There is also a well-stocked sales shop with another Trapp innovation. The instructors double as sales personnel as well as trail groomers. If you decide after your lesson that you want to make X-C a permanent part of your life, your instructor, who is familiar with you as a skier, can help you make your equipment selections.

Tracks and Trails and Tours: When asked if the trails were laid out by an old man of the mountain, Johannes von Trapp replies, "Yes. Me." Though only in his midthirties, he is old in terms of his knowledge of the thousand acres of rolling Green Mountain land surrounding the Trapp Family Lodge. (He started his explorations when he was four years old.) Johannes supervised and did much of the cutting of what is now sixty miles of trails, all of which are groomed like a Kentucky Derby winner. Johannes justly prides himself on having the best trail maintenance in the country. To help defray the not inconsiderable costs of such care, an inconsiderable charge of a dollar is made for those who want to use the trails but who are not lodge guests.

The trails are swept as well as groomed. At the end of the day the instructors ski the trails, gathering up the laggards. Consequently, it's next to impossible to be marooned in the wilderness at the Trapps'. It's also mighty tough to get lost, because all the trails are marked with large, red-lettered redwood signs, bearing such names as Telemark, Johannes Rest, Slayton Pasteur, Deer Pond, the Haul Road and Fox Track.

A pleasant easy run is the Sugar Road, which takes you around behind the hill that backs onto the Lodge and delivers you to the Gift Shop and Coffee House down the road. If you take a right off Sugar Road and go steeply up the hill, you can see the Trapps' beautiful little fieldstone chapel.

Touring at the Trapps' is also a botanical experience. They've marked the many varieties of trees—yellow birch, Eastern hemlock, pin cherry, aspen, et cetera—with identification plaques.

Scenery: Louise Hertell, the long-time manager of the Gift Shop and Coffee House, tells the story of a gentleman who came into the viewful dining room of the Coffee House. He sat there hour after hour until she grew worried that he might be ill. She asked if there were anything she could do for him. He sighed and said, "No, I hope you don't mind my sitting here. I'd like to stay a little longer. You see, I'm from near Salzburg, Austria. I'm terribly homesick and this reminds me so much of home . . ." These Vermont hills *are* very similar to Salzburgerland, but even if they remind you of nothing, they are lovely enough on their own to start new memories. It's a pattern of hills beyond hills, streams, woods, meadows all put together like a giant well-ordered park planned by a master landscape architect.

A further convincing report from Louise Hertell is of a ten-year-old boy, a breed not notorious for its highly developed sense of natural aesthetics. He came in for lunch after a tour and with eyes glistening like snow in sunshine said to her, "Lady, do you know how *beautiful* it is out there?"

Accommodations and Cuisine: The Lodge itself is an authentic Austrian chalet, complete with balconies all around on every level and a bell tower. It is all wood, outside cedar, inside white pine, and as the temperature fluctuates—there's lots of freeze and thaw in Vermont—the wood of the house sings like a member of the family chorus. There are three fireplaces. One is in the St. George Room, a kind of recreation area. Another is in the living room, which was the Trapp family living room when this was strictly their home back in the early forties. The third is downstairs in the Tirolerstueberl bar, which nightly pours forth the sound of Austrian accordian music. The family chalet began its career as a lodge back in the fifties and now includes two annexes across the road. The Trapps can accommodate a hundred twenty guests in rooms ranging from small and simple to large and elegant.

If you read Maria von Trapp's book, *The Story of the Trapp Family Singers,* you will get an insight into the struggles that went into building the house. All the family members hacked out the hardpan by hand to make the cellar, and Maria haunted auctions to discover such treasures as the statues of the Apostles that are on the living room mantle beneath the portrait of Baron Georg von Trapp, who died in 1947.

The menu at the Lodge bears the legend, "*Gesegnete Mahlezeit*" or "Blessed Repast." And you feel blessed to be able to partake of it. On the modified American plan you can select what you will from the menu, and you will want to select Austrian specialties, such as *Wienerschnitzel* and *Wiener Zwiebel Rostbraten* and the neighboring specialty, spicy Hungarian goulash (order with this a bottle of Hungarian Egribikajer, "bull's blood" wine). You can get these specialties adorned with homemade noodles (*Spätzli*) or dumplings (*Knödel*).

Then there's dessert so absolutely knockout delicious you feel like following the childhood scheme of eating dessert first to make sure you have room for it. There's a choice of *Schwarzwälder Kirschtorte* (cherry brandy cake), *Haselnusstorte* (hazel nut cake), Apple Strudel, or everyone's favorite, *Linzertorte* made of ground nuts and jam.

Another Trapp family surprise. The chef who puts together all these Salzburg sensations is not Austrian but American. Johannes, who is himself the only American-born member of the family, says it works better to take a good even-tempered American chef and teach him the family recipes than it does to take a temperamental European chef and suffer his tantrums.

Ambiance: If you liked *The Sound of Music,* you'll be enchanted by the Trapp Family Lodge. But even if you're of the Pauline Kael school of film criticism and consider the technicolor version of life with the Trapps to have too much sugar to be your cup of tea, you'll still be enchanted by the place. If you ask the old Mona Lisa question, "Are you warm, are you real?" of the Trapp Family Lodge, there is no possible answer but yes. From the *Cor Unum* (one heart) name of the house over the door to the admonition above the reception desk of "Do unto others as though *You* were the others," to the family mementos and religious carvings that adorn the walls to the small family cemetery out behind the house, everything adds up to genuine humanness. Nothing at the Trapps' is done for show or studied effect. Everything is what it seems.

Much of the spirit of the place has to come from Maria, who still makes the Lodge her home. Even after all the fame generated by her romanticized portrayal in the Julie Andrews movie, she remains the same sincere, unaffected person. Yet she is not by any means a cream puff. She is a woman of strength and magnetism. As one staff member says, "Look at her eyes. She has something very special to give to those who are ready to receive it." You could say the same of the whole Trapp family operation.

7. THE GRAND TOUR

In the eighteenth century the Grand Tour of Europe was the crowning of a young gentleman's learning. It was, as Anthony Burgess says in his introduction to *The Grand Tour,* "an education of the flesh and the spirit at one and the same time."

So it is for the X-C-er. A Grand Tour of Europe can be the cap and the culmination of your skinny ski education. It is a double-threat combination. It is grand in both the great and the glorious sense. It is a tour in both the ski and the see sense. Put them all together and you have everything the flesh and the spirit of a ski tourer could ask for.

THE ALPS

When you do X-C for the fun of it, the peripherals count as much as the basic process. That's why ski touring in the

Alps is such a wonderful experience. The Alps are loaded with pleasurable peripherals. What makes it all the better is that you get the pleasurable peripherals of four national cultures: Austria, France, Italy, and Switzerland.

It is easy to get to the Alps. The downhillers have blazed the trail for us with lots of charters and bargain flights and package tours which include flights, transfers, hotels, and meals. The hoteliers and restaurateurs and shopkeepers of the Alps are experienced and ready to make visitors comfortable and happy. The after-ski life, when downhillers and tourers and all nationalities come together, is a celebration of *Gemütlichkeit, joie de vivre,* and *Mamma mia!*

The Alpine resorts are also several diagonal strides ahead of us in ski touring facilities. They got the X-C bug a few seasons before we did. A glance at the Appendix will show you which Alpine resorts have developed touring tracks (*loipen*) and trails.

Most of these resorts have long well-marked-and-maintained tracks that weave in and out around the resort, usually taking you by the best sights and scenery often through woods and along streams. Since the higher slopes are usually reserved for downhillers, the areas used for cross-country are relatively flat with only a few easily negotiated humps and hummocks. You seldom if ever have to worry about getting lost on these tracks, if you stick to them, that is. Naturally, you can get yourself lost almost anywhere, if you set your mind to it.

There are always more than plenty little places to stop in for your coffee or wine break or lunch, so you don't necessarily have to tote everything on your back. Of course, you may want to tote anyway, because there are also always more than plenty little shops vending the crusty fresh rolls and chunks of tangy cheese and regionally distinctive cold meats and salamis and bottles of *vin ordinaire* that don't taste at all *ordinaire* when you sip them trackside after your lope on the *loipe.*

Another advantage of X-C in the Alps is that as in the United States it gets you away from the crowds. Only more so. At least in the States, if you go midweek to a resort, you can find some small measure of privacy. It's not that easy in the Alps. Europeans tend to take more long winter holidays than we do, and there are a lot of Europeans around to take them. Add to them all of us Americans, especially east coast Americans, who love to zap over to sample the perpendiculars and peripherals, and you have yourself a gang queuing up for the lifts. But not, mercifully, a gang gliding the trails.

Ski touring is the ideal way to explore one or several of the Alpine countries. Doing downhill it sometimes takes you a week to learn the lifts and runs. In contrast, you can immediately find the X-C *loipe* and take off. Consequently, in two or three days you can make that area yours and move on to conquer and savor another. X-C equipment is also lighter and easier to sling onto a train or on top of a car and hoist on your shoulder and walk to the hotel.

There is so much touring to be done in the Alps that you could easily follow the example of the young gentlemen of the eighteenth century and devote a year to it. If you have somewhat less time than that, you must pick and choose.

Here are a few personal signposts to help you plan your X-C Grand Tour.

AUSTRIA

`Why Austria? Austria is the essence of the Alps in scenery and architecture and music. It's picturesque in the very best and most authentic and unphony sense of the word. Thanks to the people with their buoyant and humorous outlook on life, it's the happiest feeling of the Alpine countries.

Where in Austria? Without hesitation, it's Kitzbühel. If Austria is the essence of the Alps, Kitz is the essence of Austria. It is without qualification one of the most charming villages that snow ever fell upon. It just has one little problem. The sun also shines upon it and a warm wind often blows upon it and occasionally and unseasonably sometimes even rain falls upon it. All these inappropriate happenings tend to louse up the snow, sending the downhillers fleeing to higher territory. Let them flee. The X-C-er can stay and wax appropriately and ski happily on the loused-up snow. So much the better, because then he'll have the medieval beauty of the town and the grandeur of the mountains and the whipped cream and zither music all to himself.

Now for a word about the *loipen* on which to do the *Langlauf* and the *Skiwandern*. The word is plenty. There are prepared and marked tracks of 1, 3, 6, 10, and 14 kilometers. Should that not be enough for your greedy appetite, in nearby St. Johann in Tirol there are 5, 10, and 15-

kilometer tracks. Do you hunger for more? More there is in still nearer-by Kirchberg. Here you can find 20 kilometers of tracks for your touring pleasure plus two-hour guided tours every morning and afternoon except Sunday. Kitzbühel, in other words, is the kind of place you can settle into for a long stay with little danger of boredom setting in.

There are hotels in abundance, but since there are also skiers in abundance, you need to make your reservations early. If money is no object in your choice of accommodations, then the only place to stay is the Postkutsche. The name means "carriage house," and indeed it is most suitable for the carriage trade. Its atmosphere could be called either intimate grandeur or palatial coziness. Its cuisine could be called *Holiday* Magazine Award-Winning, because that's what it is.

Much more reasonably priced is the fifty-room Schweizerhof, but you'll probably have a heckuva time wrestling a room away from the downhiller pack, because it's almost on top of the Hahnenkammbahn lift station. Other good fairly reasonable stops are the Guido Reisch and the Jagerwirt. But even if you have to resort to curling up under the archway that the main street runs under, it's worth it just to be in this delightful and increasingly X-C-conscious Tyrolean town.

FRANCE

Why France? Well, I guess just because it's so militantly and unremittently French. It's the sardonic citizens, who haven't yet and never will recognize English as the new international language. It's the pungent smells of the trains and streets. It's the absolutely unmatchable-anywhere-in-the-world cuisine. But most of all, it's that *je ne sais quoi* of France that has hooked us Americans all the way back to Benjamin Franklin.

Where in France? Autrans near Grenoble, in its quaint French way, calls itself France's *Foyer de Ski de Fond. Ski de fond,* which loosely translates as "endurance skiing," is the French term for cross-country racing. The more relaxed form of the sport that we pursue they refer to as *ski de promenade,* which needs no translation. What we call ski mountaineering the French call *ski de randonnée* or "the ski of the long circuit."

Actually, Autrans is a *foyer* of anything you want to do on touring skis. They have some fifty kilometers of tracks and trails as a result of having the natural terrain—a series of limestone plateaus—plus the man-made embellishments created to make them the Nordic events center for the 1968 Winter Olympics. Autrans is also the training center for the French Nordic team.

The one thing that Autrans lacks is a first-class hotel. The best they have to offer are La Terrasse and the Poste, both of which fall into the *Guide Michelin's* "plain but fairly comfortable" category. If you require the "very comfortable" category, Villard de Lans, only 14 kilometers away, can provide you with three: La Pelissière and Christiania, both of which count among their comforts a heated pool, and the Eterlou, which has an exceptional view to make up for its lack of the waterworks. Although

Villard de Lans is not quite the *ski de fond foyer* that Autrans is, it shares the same sunny plateau terrain. It offers plenty of trails to keep you busy, including some higher mountain "ski of the long circuit" that you'd be best advised to hire a *moniteur spécialisé* (guide who specializes in ski touring) to lead the way to and, more important, to lead the way back from.

Grenoble is the handy gateway to these two X-C centers, but if you want to come down heavier on the fun of it than on the run of it, then land instead in Geneva, Switzerland, and head south to Megève, France. Megève is located in a wide-open valley. It's one of the oldest resorts in France, having been built up from an already established mountain village by the Rothschilds back in the days before all us peasants got involved with snow sports. As a result, the buildings in Megève are stone-solid and oozing atmosphere rather than the ticky-tacky or the starkly modern you find in some of the French Jean-come-lately resorts.

Although in Megève there are no marked race courses for the intense *ski de fond* practitioners, there are plenty of places in the sun to do your *ski de promenade*. You can chug up from the base of the Mt. d'Arbois lift to La Planellet and Le Mas and on beyond as far as your legs will allow. Or you can do the same kind of gentle wandering climb up from the Rochebrune lift terminal to Le Tour. You can also slide around to your heart's content down in the valley with little fear of getting lost too far from home.

There are a lot of homes in Megève that you wouldn't want to get too far from. One with only thirteen guest rooms, the Gérentière, makes up for its size with a *Guide*

Michelin star restaurant. (Oh, that mountain trout brought to the table still flipping in the net for your inspection and, oh, that paprika chicken.) It also has a notable guest book, including such luminous names as Peter Sellers and Roger Vadim with his Galatea of the moment.

Another *Michelin* star restaurant is in the Mont-Joly Hotel, where they have a few more rooms (twenty-six) and a few less francs on your bill. The Hermitage up on the road to Mt. d'Arbois is a fifty-two room wine-lover's paradise with its 16,000-bottle cellar.

Should you want more variety in your Megève *ski de promenade,* you can find it in another picturesque village, St. Gervais, only eleven kilometers away. Here you have a big, woodsy park with trails to ramble.

ITALY

Why Italy? There's the warm sunshine and the equally warm people. There's the beauty of the Dolomites, which to my mind are the outstanding scenery mountains in the world. They are like no others with their flat-topped peaks and their layers of red and orange that make them look like Grand Canyons in the sky. There are also fewer American tourists in the Italian resorts than in any of the other Alpine countries.

Where in Italy? I'd say Cortina in thunder. Be ye not scared off by the superchic image of Cortina portrayed in the movie *The Pink Panther.* The jetsetters and noble names are there, yes. Give them credit for sniffing out the best and the most beautiful. But don't let reverse snobbery keep you away from a good thing. Besides, it's part of the fun to watch them stalk the streets wearing their finery and their disdainful expressions.

Cortina is definitely not the wallet buster you might expect it to be, especially since the dollar didn't tumble as far down the cellar stairs in Italy as it did in the other Alpine countries. Besides, you don't have to stay in a deluxe palazzo of the likes of the Miramonti Majestic. There is the first-class, total comfort, and heart-of-the-town convenience yet lack of expense of the Parc Hotel Victoria and one small step down, the older, more homely and homey charm of the Regina. These hotels usually require that you eat all your meals in. You might prefer the freedom of one of the two garnis (bed and breakfast only): the Olimpia and the Montana. If you do, be sure to try at least one meal at the Foghèr. This restaurant is an unfancy and inexpensive but unsurpassable dispensary of the best of northern Italian cuisine.

In Italian, X-C is called *sci di fondo,* and the practitioners of it go by the dramatic-sounding appellation *fondisti.* In Cortina make your *sci di fondo* skimming excursions all over the lower levels of the slopes, but when you want to race along the official track, you should go out on the Belluno–Venice road near the Miramonti. This track makes a great circle around the ski jump erected for the 1956 Olympics. Another Olympic dividend is the huge ice rink on the other end of town, which you can apply yourself to should your muscles still be twitching for additional activity between the end of the touring and the start of the *dolce notte.*

An Italian alternate resort to Cortina is Ortisei or Sankt Ulrich, depending on whether it's going by its Italian or its German name. They use both languages in these parts, since the area once belonged to Austria. Actually, going to Ortisei gives you the flavor of both Austria and Italy for the price of one. Ortisei is one of the complex of resorts in the Val Gardena area and is extremely easy to reach. It's only nineteen miles from Bressanone, the gateway to the Brenner Pass.

As for hotels, the Aquila, although not luxurious, is the tops in price and convenience, but my personal favorite is the more intimate Villa Emilia up on the hill with a fine view of the valley and the Dolomites and with a cuisine to match the view.

Ortisei is the wood-carving capital of the Italian Alps—and maybe in the world. It seems that every other citizen practices the art, and you can see examples in the shops all over town. For my money (literally) the best is David Moroder, whose studio is only a few blocks from the Villa Emilia and who won the competition for the carving to be placed outside the city hall.

Where you should do your *sci* thing is up, way up on the sun-soaked plateau of Alpè di Siusi. Take the cable car from Ortisei and there you are and there it is—a gigantic snowy garden of the Gods sprouting jagged red peaks. There are some gentle downhill runs up there, but they are unobtrusive and they will melt out of sight as you glide around the mild terrain, making your own tracks and trails or (carefully, very carefully) following the paths used by the horse-drawn sleighs.

There is at Alpè di Siusi one of the best hotels in the area, the Eurotel Sciliar. Although I think it's more fun to be down in Ortisei, where you can do some after-ski shop-hopping, the Sciliar makes a marvelous and viewful lunch stop.

SWITZERLAND

Why Switzerland? The Swiss are the past and present masters of tourism. If you cannot find total contentment lodging with the solicitous Swiss, you are a chronic curmudgeon. It is not without reason that Switzerland is the world's favorite winter vacation land. The Swiss Alps are the highest and most spectacular in Europe. What a joy it is to ski around gazing up at them with the realization that you can enjoy them without risking your bones on them.

Where in Switzerland? The enthusiasm for X-C is running high in all parts of the country. Here is where the nonwaxer's delight, the mohair strip-bottomed skis, were invented and where the "Langläufer Leben Länger" motto was coined. To my mind, however, the section of Switzerland that best combines X-C with those pleasurable peripherals of Europe is the area south and east of Zürich that is known as the Grisons, or, in German, the Grabünden. In this section you will find Arosa, Davos, Klosters, and Flims and in all of these you will find generously laid-out, well-maintained, and scenic *loipen,* as well as quantities of gracious hotels.

In the Grisons you will also find St. Moritz. Here I go again recommending an international luxury resort for our humble, self-effacing sport of ski touring. It just seems to work out that way in the Alps. These are the resorts with the wide-open spaces, sunshine, and glorious scenery and the enterprise to develop all facets of winter sports including X-C. St. Moritz has it all and has more and better than most. There is probably no more beautiful and exhilarating X-C track in the Alps than the one running across the frozen St. Moritzersee from which you can look up to see St. Moritz leaning against the mountainside below the Corviglia ski slopes. This track is a portion of the path of the twenty-five-mile Engadine Ski Marathon, which is run from Maloja to Zuoz every March. This is a race that, as they say in the announcement, would delight Avery Brundage, since it is an unquestionably amateur contest. One look at the five thousand participants will convince you of that. All ages and conditions enter. It is an honorable thing just to participate and it is a notable achievement just to finish, whatever the time it takes.

St. Moritz is another resort replete with hotel beds—about twenty thousand of them—both in the center of town and out in the outskirts and suburbs. In St. Moritz Dorf, which is what you think of when you think of St. Moritz, there are three central hotels that are excellent and not exorbitant, at least not by St. Moritz standards of exorbitance. These are the Albana, the Neues Posthotel (splendid restaurant), and the slightly more expensive Monopol with its penthouse swimming pool. All three have inspiring views of the X-C track on the lake, if you pay the extra tariff for the view side, that is. A good second-class central location house is the Bernasconi.

A less-expensive alternate to St. Moritz proper would be to stay in one of the outlying areas and skim in and out of Dorf on the X-C track. A particularly hearty recommendation for this method of operations would be Pontresina where, besides the run to St. Moritz, there are eight marked and curried X-C trails through the Swiss stone pine woods.

Window-shopping is a favorite activity in St. Moritz. While indulging in this pastime, you'll notice a wide selection of stylish cross-country attire, vividly demonstrating the fact that X-C is being taken up by the smart set. But be not dismayed. To mix a floral metaphor, the lily of X-C, even as gilded in St. Moritz, is still as sweet a sport.

NORWAY

Remember what a wonderful place the world used to be? It still is in Norway. Going there is like a trip backward in time to when the air was clean and the land was uncrowded and family members enjoyed each other's company.

Norway is such a beautiful country with such warm and winning people that you'd want to go there, even if they hadn't invented cross-country skiing. And it has such fabulous X-C facilities that you'd want to take advantage of them, even if the rest of the countryside were composed of nothing but strip mining and pig farms, and the people were all waspish.

As it is, with its combination of superpositive elements, Norway is total perfection for a ski touring holiday. After all, where it all began is where you'd expect to find it at its apogee.

CINDERELLA STEPS OUT: As you do cross-country skiing at home and abroad, you're bound to notice one thing. Ski touring is the stepsister of downhill. Alpine skiing gets the attention and the facilities, and X-C gets the leftovers and hand-me-downs. Everywhere but in Norway, that is. In Norway X-C is skiing and skiing is X-C. Slalom is that other thing that young hotshots and visiting British do. Instead of a ski resort having a token X-C track or trail set at the base of a dozen lifts, in Norway it's the other way around. They have a token lift or two with downhill runs set among miles and miles and miles of well-maintained touring trails.

It's refreshing to see X-C running the snow sports show, and you can't help but notice that it's a more benevolent ruler than downhill usually is.

EVERYBODY'S DOING IT: Nowhere else can you witness the all-ages and all-conditions universal appeal of ski touring that is in evidence in Norway. It's fun just to stand beside a trail and watch the passing parade. There are elderly women skiing along gossiping. There are young marrieds pulling their tiny—some under six months—babies in pulkas, those sleds that are hauled with long stiff poles rather like those attached to horses in harness races. There are people out with their dogs on leashes, and it's hard to tell who's having a better time or who's pulling whom. One particularly memorable sight in Lillehammer was a lean, ascetic-faced young man with a beard skiing along with two Russian wolfhounds in tow.

There are solitary skiers, both men and women, young and old, out for their after-work constitutionals. There are children of all ages, including those so young as to not quite have the hang of walking yet. There are iron-jawed, iron-haired men who race along with visions of their former days of running the Birkebeiner or Vasaloppet dancing in their heads. There is, in fact, a perfect cross-section of the population with the generation gap so tightly sealed that you can't even see its seams.

A LITTLE LIGHT ON THE SUBJECT: When I planned my early March excursion to Norway, everyone clucked his tongue over the fact that in such a northern latitude I would probably be doing most of my skiing in the pitch dark. So often did I hear this that I began to worry myself. As it turned out, having enough daylight hours was the least of my worries (the *very* least, considering the fact that I was there during a dollar devaluation and closed money market period).

I can assure you that the Land of the Midnight Sun in summer is definitely not the Land of the Noon Moon in winter. In the first week in March I noticed very little difference in the Norwegian daylight allotment from the measure I was getting back home, and I'm from California, *Southern* California.

Here are the official Oslo Travel Association's daylight hour averages by month so you can figure how many hours of light you need to glide the trails and schedule your trip accordingly.

MONTH	NUMBER OF HOURS OF DAYLIGHT
November	7–9
December	6–7
January	6–8
February	8–10
March	10–13
April	13–16

OF BOOZE AND BOARDS: A couple of complications I didn't expect, however, do exist in Norway. The first of these is spiritual—neutral spiritual. The hours of drink service in Norway don't make sense, or, rather, they make perfect sense, if you're striving for a sober population, as the Norwegian government must be. Now hear this: no hard liquor is available for purchase by drink or by bottle on Saturdays, Sundays, or holidays, or before three o'clock on any other day. Consequently, if you want to whoop it up by tossing it down, best you pick up your allotment at the tax-free shop in your takeoff airport. Even if you're a very moderate drinker, you might want to take something along, anyway, because the Norwegian government further encourages sobriety by slapping on such heavy liquor taxes that all things alcoholic—even wine and beer—are about double what they are back in the land of repealed prohibition.

More surprising than the liquor laws and costs, though, is the unavailability of skis for rental. In all of Oslo there is one (!) place to rent skis. That's Tomm Murstad's out of the high rent district on the next-to-last stop of the Holmenkollenbahn.

Not only are rental skis hard to find, but the only ones available are those with cable bindings. (A shop attendant told me this is because they are more easily adjusted to different foot sizes.) Consequently, if you bring along your boots, and not your skis, as I did, your boots are just taking up luggage space, because they won't work with the kind of bindings that are available and you wind up renting boots, too. Therefore, take all or nothing at all in terms of equipment.

I most heartily recommend all. Having to seek—and maybe seek in vain—a place to rent equipment is a horrible waste of time. You'll be happier with your own equipment. No doubt you'll already have the equipment, because Norway is more likely to be a culmination trip for someone who's done a bit of touring at home rather than the first steps of the learning experience.

Not only that, but taking X-C skis along is not that much trouble. They're light for the flight, and every—I mean *every*—Norwegian taxi has a ski rack on top, so there's no problem toting the skis to wherever you go. When you go somewhere on the train, you can drop your skis off at the baggage check room (*reisegodsekpedisjon*) in the station. They will be sent on the same train you're on and you can pick them up at your destination. All this convenience goes for a flat rate of 5 kroner. Also, every hotel, including the most deluxe ones in Oslo, has a ski storage room.

I've tried to analyze the mystery of why there's such a dearth of X-C ski rental shops in Norway. It's particularly puzzling when you can rent them easily in practically every Swiss resort. The reason must be because of the previously mentioned everybody's-doing-it aspect of the sport. Since in Norway everybody skis, everybody, from toddler to dodderer, owns his own equipment. Consequently, trying to rent skis in Norway is something like trying to rent a pair of tennis shoes in California. Again, I can't say it in dark-enough type: **take your own skis and boots with you to Norway.**

Thrift tips: All of us former "rich Americans" in terms of foreign travel now have to be a little more careful in dealing out our devalued dollars. One nice thing about Norway is that it's possible to figure out your costs fairly well in advance, because it is not, as are some of the more southerly nations of Europe, the land of the extended palm. Tipping is less expected than in any country I've traveled in, and that includes the United States.

You can figure your expenses ahead of time most closely and also reduce them appreciably if you buy a prepaid package tour. Both SAS and Pan Am offer these. Write them for brochures or pick them up from your travel agent.

If you prefer to do it yourself, there are still ways to trim expenses. For example, the best hotels of Oslo (Bristol, Continental, Grand, KNA, and Viking) offer an Oslo weekend package. These are valid from Friday afternoon to Monday morning. For 100 kroner per person per day you get a room with a bath and breakfast and dinner. There is also a budget weekend available at the six mission hotels for 55 kroner with bath and 45 kroner without.

In the resorts it's best to stay a minimum of five days so you can be sure to get half or full pension. This saves about $5 a day compared to buying the same meals individually. And, wow, those full pension meals! Never was the word full more appropriately applied.

The Norwegian cold table breakfast with its help-yourself-to-all-you-want display of five to seven kinds of herring, a like number of cheeses, breads of all varieties, eggs, ham, lunch meats, preserves, cereals, fruits, salads —yes, salads—and the best coffee in the world is a totally unrivaled skier-stoker. Lunch is often another vaster cold table, adding shrimp and crab and smoked salmon and tongue and rare roast beef plus a big selection of hot dishes and desserts. Dinner is a more normal-sized three- or four-course affair. It's easy to see, when you're being fed in this manner, why you don't have to drop any extra kroner at snack shops to keep up your strength.

All in all, Norway is not what you'd call an inexpensive country, but then neither is any other country in Europe for us right now. In Norway, however, you receive full and solid value for what you pay, and the world being what it is today, that constitutes something of a rare bargain.

Trains: Let us now praise Norwegian trains. They are the only way to travel between resorts. They are high, wide, and handsome. They have comfortable reclining seats with footrests next to picture windows. There are places at the end of each car to hang your coat on a coat hanger and stack your bags so they're not overhead and underfoot. There are restrooms in every car with lights indicating whether or not they are occupied to keep you from having to make the walk in vain. No-smoking rules are rigidly enforced in cars of that name (*røyking ul-øvlig*). Usually there's a dining car and always there's an ambulatory goodie vendor. The children traveling on Norwegian trains are so well behaved and quiet you'd think they were sick, except that Norwegians all look like what they are—the fittest national group in the world. Riding on a Norwegian train you arrive at your destination feeling as if you've had a rest cure rather than an ordeal of travel. And you arrive right on time.

A tourable feast: The Norwegian term for smörgåsbord is "cold table" (*Koldtbord*). Besides being replete with the food variety of cold table, Norway is itself a gigantic cold table of ski touring. The Scandinavian National Tourist Offices (Head Office: 505 Fifth Avenue, New York, N. Y. 10017) and SAS (138-02 Queens Boulevard, Jamaica, N. Y. 11435) can both supply you with lip-smacking and saliva-stimulating brochures of the touring selections available to you. For once these organizations devoted to entrapping the tourist do not exaggerate. This is because it's pretty much impossible to overdo praise of the ski touring in Norway.

Where then to go? It's harder than choosing between the seven kinds of herring and the smoked salmon and fresh shrimp on a cold board, but my own choices for a well-balanced serving of delights are Geilo, Oslo, and Lillehammer. That way you get three kinds of communities: a resort, a city, and a village; and three kinds of touring terrain: moonscape, piny woods, and rolling meadows.

Geilo

There are several reasons for heading first to Geilo. You can get there easily by landing in Bergen. This is many people's favorite city in Norway. It might, for all it's scenic port city charm, be called the San Francisco of Norway. Then, too, landing in Bergen gives you the shortest flight from either the east or west coasts of the U.S. To my mind, anything that cuts down even five minutes on a transoceanic flight is worth doing.

Going to Geilo from Bergen also lets you take the Bergen–Oslo train line along which are the most scenically spectacular sights ever crossed by tracks.

And the final advantage of starting your Norwegian X-C experience in Geilo is that it's the easiest way, the way with the least cultural shock, to introduce yourself to Norway. This is because our English cousins have been using it as their Aspen for years. English, therefore, is everybody's second language, if not their first (the British are still coming). Geilo is also familiar feeling, because it is primarily a resort town, and resorts, be they Norwegian or Alpine or Vermontian or Coloradan, have a lot in common. If you've been to one, you are likely to feel at home in another.

Geilo is one of Norway's largest resorts, but still it is not by any means huge. Although there is some building going on, there are probably not many more than 1,350 hotel beds. They are much sought after, especially from mid-February on, so be sure to book well in advance. But don't let this full bed situation frighten you. Even when there's no room at the inn in any Geilo inn, as the situation was when I was there, the ski terrain seems deserted by any Alpine or American standards. As far as crowds are concerned, every day in Norway looks like the day after Christmas vacation is over.

There is a good bit of downhill skiing at Geilo, and that further tends to cut down the population—especially the hotshot population—on the touring trails.

HOTELS: There are several hotels where an American X-C-er who's there for the fun of it could find happiness. The Highland is conveniently located and modern. Its new addition and swimming pool should be ready this season. This is where the SAS and Pan Am tour packages put up their customers, and they've made a good choice. The Holmes is the venerable one. It's a British outpost, hence a mite more on the formal side, when it comes to attire. It's handy to the lift and the train and the bus station. The Bardøla is less convenient but modern, tasteful, extremely comfortable with swimming pool and sauna and massage facilities available for the muscle-weary. In addition it has the most fabulous of cold tables for breakfast and lunch that ever made you let out the notches in the belt of your knickers.

For a more budget-priced place, yet one with a glorious view from the dining room and homey comfort, there's the Griegs. Geilo even boasts a youth hostel and boast they should, because it's the biggest hotel in town.

Another possibility is the Ustaoset Høyfjellshotell in Ustaoset, a fifteen-minute bus ride from Geilo. The "Mountain Hotel" has the opulent air of a luxury hotel in the Italian Alps, yet the prices are almost identical to the major hotels in Geilo. It's a self-contained palazzo out in the touring fields, packed with Oriental rugs and objets d'art. Since Ustaoset has, in my opinion, some of the best and most accessible touring in the area for nonrugged types, it's nice to have it right outside the door. If you don't need a village to pace and if you bring along a few paperbacks with which to amuse yourself in case of a blizzard, the Ustaoset Høyfjellshotell could prove one of the most delightful places to stay.

All the Geilo hotels do their best to give you after-hours entertainment, scheduling Norwegian evenings with folk dancing and music, sleigh rides, discothèque and foreign cabaret nights ("Place Pigalle," et cetera), and they all have great combos from exotic spots like Czechoslovakia, Hungary, and Jugoslavia. I personally found that after a day of imbibing all that straight oxygen out on the trails my lids would slowly sink around nine o'clock, but if rocking around the clock is your bag, you can fill it to the bulging point in Geilo.

SKIING: Right in Geilo Sentrum, if you walk out the back door of the Highland Hotel, you can find yourself a fast twelve kilometers or so of relatively flat, woodsy skiing, more by far than you can find in most non-Norwegian resorts.

If you pick yourself up a *Turløyper* map in the tourist center, though, you'll note that you've seen only the mere surface of Geilo touring when you're still down on the surface of the valley floor. Geilo has sixty-two miles of well-marked trails, and most of them are out of sight in more ways than one, and there are more ways than one to approach them. The fastest approach for those staying at a Geilo hotel is to take the Geilo Taubane chairlift. Don't, by the way, get the fantods at the idea of taking a chairlift while wearing X-C skis, because on this particular lift you take your skis off and place them in the rack provided for them. They stop the chair when you get on and when you get off. Nothing could be easier or more comfortable, because you ride up sideways and in very cold weather they put up a canvas windscreen.

At the top of the Geilo Taubane there's a cafeteria with a panoramic view and lots of delicious skier fodder, including those superb Norwegian Danish pastries that are called, as they are all over Scandinavia, *Wienerbrød* (Vienna bread).

To get to the touring trails and avoid the downhill runs that also feed off this lift, go up the hill behind the cafeteria and turn left. There spread out below and beyond is an open plateau in the sky with a ribbon of trail stretching out into the nowhere. Actually it isn't really nowhere that it stretches to. If you follow it for 4.3 kilometers you reach Skayrandhytta, 2.6 more and you're at Prestholseter, and eventually, 5.6 kilometers more to be exact, at Ustaoset. I wouldn't advise setting off on a long trek like that without a guide, however, unless you're a survival artist with full equipment on your back. A white-out, and they happen suddenly in the changeable mountaintop weather, could leave you helplessly and hopelessly confused.

A shorter and safer tour would be to head out the trail and then turn to the right circling the base of the mountain (there are a lot of cabins there, so you feel help is always handy) to the base of the Arneliften and Fjellheisen lifts. From there you can head back to town, but the trail is a little downhill steep for my taste. I prefer to take the route back again to the Geilo Taubane and ride it down. It involves a little climbing, but what the heck, that's 50 percent of the ski touring process and it's great for appetite-whetting.

Still, given my true touring druthers in the Geilo area, I'd hop the town bus that goes up to Ustaoset. The schedule is posted at the train station, which is also the bus's point of departure. For some reason unknown to this non-Norwegian speaker, the bus says "Rutebil" on the destination sign in front. A fifteen-minute ride gets you to Ustaoset. Then it's just a matter of crossing the road and going through a tunnel under the railroad tracks. There you are—the vast open, deserted, treeless moonscape of the Hardanger mountain plateau. You feel as you step off onto the trail that you are taking that one giant step for mankind, except that it seems a little less crowded in Ustaoset than it does on the moon.

The two trails that fork off are marked with tall twigs set in the snow. You can take either and should eventually take both. They are very gentle with only enough hypothyroid mole hills along the way to keep you interested. The flatness is not surprising when you consider you're skiing the frozen Lake Uste. On these trails leading out from Ustaoset you can race along with tremendous ease. You'll probably never feel more competent and confident than you do here.

For the hardies there's the opportunity to strike out uphill and go for broke on the four-mile trail to Ustetind, a 4,500-foot peak. Or on the opposite side of the road you can take the reverse route and climb back to Geilo. You wind up at the Geilo Taubane lift. But, again, these are no routes for the inexperienced or unprepared or solitary skier.

Geilo's trails will probably exhaust you before you exhaust them, but however it works out, the time will come when you have to get back on the train for the other half of the Bergen–Oslo run.

Oslo

Think what it would be like if Kitzbühel were on the outskirts of Vienna or if Cortina were a suburb of Rome or if Autrans were only a few Métro stops from the heart of Paris. This beautiful state of affairs exists in Norway, where on three sides of the capital city there are touring trails in the Oslomarka, 1,250 miles of them to be exact. You can sling your skis onto the back rack of a bus or side rack of a subway car and take off.

The beautiful corollary of this is that you don't *have* to sling your skis on anything and go anywhere. Should the weather be bad or a muscle be sore, you don't have to flail yourself into action. (Commandment for those who X-C for the fun of it: Thou shalt not flail thyself.) If you feel like it, you can declare this Kon Tiki and Viking Ship seeing day. Or Sonja Henie–Neils Onstad Museum seeing day. Or Vigeland Sculpture in Frogner Park day. Or Munch Museum day. Or Resistance Museum day in the Akershus Fortress. Or strolling and shopping on Karl Johan day. The possibilities are as limitless as the ski trails out in the Oslomarka.

To realize the full extent of the possibilities, pick up an SAS City Portrait of Oslo, available in all SAS offices in this country and abroad. These city guides tell everything you need to know about everything from arrival to zoos. As a matter of fact, if you are the brazen type, try to nab as many of these sixty-eight different City Portraits as you can for cities all over the world, including the major ones in the United States. Putting them all together you have yourself a world guide book that is more valuable than most of those sold at heavy prices.

HOTELS: The best hotels for your intents and purposes in Oslo are those within a short walk of the Holmenkollen Railway, the thirty-minute electric train link to the ski parks. In the top categories, that would be the Continental, which is virtually roosting on the station entrance, and the Grand, only a couple of blocks away. Down just one step in luxe is the KNA. Others that are less expensive yet still convenient are the Nobel and the Savoy.

Or if you want a magnificent view of the Oslo Fjord and would rather make your headquarters near the skiing action, stay at the Holmenkollen Turisthotel located near the ski jump, just twenty minutes outside of town by the electric train.

Dining in Oslo offers great possibilities, too. My favorite is the Blom, the artists' restaurant with its central splashing fountain and its walls lined with imaginative coats-of-arms of famous entertainers and a piano tinkling out the song hits of the thirties, forties, and fifties. Try their ptarmigan (wood grouse) in cream with cranberry sauce.

Other outstanding restaurants are Frascati, Fregatten, some call this the best seafood restaurant in the world, and Najaden out by the Kon Tiki. Do not ignore your hotel dining room, either. These definitely do not offer the characterless blahs which hotels catering to an international clientele tend to serve in an attempt not to startle anyone's palate. The dining rooms in Oslo's major hotels are elegant, the food is wonderful (try the venison or trout), and the prices not as high as you would expect for what you get.

SKIING: Everyone always heads out on the Holmenkollenbahn for their first Oslo touring experience, and so did I. (The train costs 3.25 kroner and you pay the conductor on the inside when he comes around to collect.) I stopped at the next-to-last station, Voksenkollen, and trotted across the tracks to rent skis and perforce boots from Tomm Murstad's shop.

Working in the shop was either an Englishman who spoke flawless Norwegian or a Norwegian who spoke flawless British English. He was also, it turned out, either a fantastic skier who could not conceive of anyone having less skill then he or he was a sadist.

Taking advantage of his linguistic skills, I started grilling him on the best trails to take. I had already worked over the hall porter in the hotel, and he had told me the easiest trail was the one which circled around the TV tower, an easy spot to find, since the Tryvannstarnet is the highest observation tower in Scandinavia with a 5,000-square-mile view.

Tomm Murstad's man advised a couple of different trails, which led off from the left as you face the shop. When I asked him about the one around the Tryvann Tower, he made a face and said, "That is the most crowded trail in Norway and the most boring trail in the world."

"But," I whined, "aren't those two trails off to the left kind of downhill? Wouldn't they be a little tough to handle in this snow?" (It was hardpack with little ice runners for ski tracks.)

"No," he assured me. "You won't have a bit of trouble if you can ski at all."

That got to me. After all, I do have some pride. I had some wax painted onto my skis for 4 kroner. (Most of the

Norwegians, I noticed, were having it done for them too.) Then I set off. I had not gone ten yards before I began to have serious doubts. There was nothing to do, at least there was nothing I could do to try to check my speed but snowplow, and I couldn't even do that very well on the marble surface with no appreciable edges on my skis.

After the first minor horror hill there was a flat run through the trees, and I got my first whiff of how beautiful Oslo skiing can be. There was a double-tracked trail through the clean-smelling woods. You could ski along side-by-side with companions and chat.

But this beautiful respite was soon over. I should have taken the warning, when a crusty old Norwegian came stomping back on foot. I asked him how it was up ahead. He put it succinctly, "Impossible!"

Still I persisted in my folly. The Murstad wax job was so superb that I leaped up the icy hill like a jackrabbit, just as fast and as well, I thought, as the Norwegians. The wax job was just as superb (alas!) on the steep downhill. I found myself skiing twice as fast and ten times worse than the Norwegians. It was complete lack of control and total terror. As I leaned trembling against a tree, one Norwegian girl whose boy friend had taken her out skiing, apparently against her better judgment, moaned in English through clenched teeth, "I just *detest* this." So, I decided, did I. After about an hour and a half of delightful climbs and horrifying descents, I called it a bad show, took off my skis, and hiked back to Murstad's.

The British-Norwegian expert-sadist was no longer on duty. A not-so-fluent but much more kindhearted boy was. I thought he was going to cry when I told him I was going to have to turn in my skis because I couldn't handle the skiing.

"Oh, you can't do that," he said and proceeded to haltingly direct me up the hill from the shop (you walk up a path to the right, then put on your skis at the top) to the runs I'd wanted in the first place, the Skjennungsvannet (3.5 kilometers), the Tryvannstua (3 kilometers), and the Nordmarkaskoppellot (6 kilometers).

Since it was a sunny Sunday, there was lots of snow play going on in the open area at the top, and the trail that led off from it was a little crowded in Norwegian terms, but it wasn't at all bad in any other national terms you could mention. It was easy, gentle, up and down skiing through the woods with occasional spectacular views of the Oslo Fjord shining dark gold against a light gold sky. Especially memorable was the sight from up near the Tryvann Tower, where I stopped for a *solbartoddy* (hot blackberry punch).

Not that in good snow the other runs all over the Nordmarka wouldn't be wonderful touring. And the snow is usually pretty wonderful. I just happened to be there in the warmest winter in forty years. Still, if you do ski the trails around the more mountainous parts, just be sure you have your snowplow down pat.

Besides the runs around the TV tower, another favorite for us more casual types is the 5-kilometer trail out to Ullevalseter from Sognsvann. To get there you take the Sognsvann train, which leaves from the same station as the Holmenkollenbahn, and ride to the end of the line.

This is a completely nonmountainous run alongside—or over—a lake. There's a restaurant at the end of the trail where you can have a relaxed lunch and ski back. A good day's outing.

This is, of course, just a nibble at the edge of Oslo's skiing. Be sure to get a list of the main trails at the tourist office. Then make your own selections from the possibilities of the Nordmarka, Sognsvann, Lillomarka, and Østmarka.

BADGES OF DISTINCTION: If you stay in Oslo long enough, or if you happen to be indefatigable, you can earn a distance badge: 100 kilometers for a bronze, 250 for a silver, and 500 for a gold. This is not done on the honor system the way the U. S. distance badges (see Appendix) are. There are check points all over the Oslomarka where you get your control card stamped to prove your kilometerage.

Incidentally, as evidence that you can't beat an American when it comes to fanaticism, an American colonel stationed in Norway, a man who had never previously skied before in his life, racked up 2,237 kilometers in one season. He earned four gold badges for his efforts. His piker wife only earned two.

Lillehammer

I know intellectually that the Bergen–Oslo line has the most beautiful train window scenery in Norway, but in my heart's eye the two-and-a-half-hour Oslo–Lillehammer run wins out. Not long after you leave the city's West station you begin to see the birch trees that look as if their trunks were wound with silver ribbons. The boulders along the way are a light gray with a pink cast in the sun.

Then the train starts its run beside the charcoal-gray waters of Lake Mjøsa, Norway's largest, and it looks like a good-size match for Japan's Inland Sea. Where the lake is frozen along the edges you see fishermen at the quiet vigil beside their ice fishing holes. Almost every house you pass has a matching bird house. Hospitality for all in Norway.

Then you're chugging into Lillehammer station. One of the nicest things about Lillehammer is that it's a real town with real people doing real-life things. It's not just a resort or a tourist center. No matter how lovely tourist centers may be, they always have a slight essence of the artificial about them.

Although Lillehammer has twenty thousand bodies and souls on the record books, it seems much more small-town, even village-like than that. The people are relaxed and friendly and helpful the way small-town people are. For example, when I went in to rent skis at the Helleberg Sports Shop, since they didn't have any light touring skis with bindings that fitted my boots, they mounted new bindings on the rental skis at no extra charge.

Lillehammer is just the right size for strolling. It's small enough to be manageable, yet big enough to have a variety of things to see, including a new art gallery (Lillehammer has been a center for artists since the turn of the century), the home of Sigrid Undset (from the outside only), and dozens of shops featuring sporting goods and Norwegian sweaters. Look for the yarn shop on the Storgata. It has handknits for less than any other shop I saw in Norway. Beautiful hand-carved pipes are a Lillehammer specialty. As in most Norwegian towns of any size, there's a branch of Husfliden, the government-operated store that sells all kinds of Norwegian handicrafts.

At night there are movies and concerts in the new modern theater as well as the usual resort features of sleigh rides, ice skating, and dancing in all the hotels to combos alternating soft nostalgia with hard rock.

HOTELS: An American tourer can find plenty of comfort and entertainment in the hotels of Lillehammer. You couldn't go wrong with the Kronen, the Lillehammer Turisthotel, the Oppland, or the Victoria. Up on the Nordseter (about which *much* more later) there is another generous selection, including the star of the mountain, the Nevra, which you could call the Ustaoset Mountain Hotel of the Nordseter because of its spacious, opulent elegance and its right-on-top-of-the-trails location.

One thing you won't find in Lillehammer is another American tourist. In my entire stay there I saw only one young American couple—he, beard; she, long straight hair; both, jeans and backpacks. They were sitting confused in a konditori waiting for a waitress who would never come. (The protocol in these places is: make your selection of *Wienerbrød* or *smørbrød* at the counter, order your drink, pay for everything, sit down, and it will be brought to you.)

You won't find the British in Lillehammer, either. They seem to favor the closer-to-them resorts along the Bergen–Oslo line. Just about all you will find in Lillehammer are Norwegians, who, from a lifetime of experience, know how to pick a place to ski tour.

SKIING: If you're staying at a hotel in town, you'll be awakened by the village church clock striking forty. A look out the window at the orange sherbet sunrise will confirm that it's going to be another beautiful day. Lillehammer is noted in Norway for its benign and steady climate. A Norway Travel Association booklet claims there are twenty days of sunshine on an average each winter month.

Then it's into your knickers and down to the breakfast groaning board. Your hotel probably provides a bus ride up to the Nordseter, but if it doesn't, there's one leaving on a regular schedule at 4 kroner a ride from the train station. It stops for more passengers at the square in front of the Hotel Kronen.

Nine miles up the hill and you reach the Nordseter. I couldn't believe it the first time I saw it. If God opened a ski touring center in Heaven, it would be exactly like the Nordseter. The Lillehammer tourist brochure says the Nordseter "was originally a summer hill farm but it has developed into a tourist center because of its natural significance." That's an understatement on a par with that of the hotel hall porter, who, when I asked where the ski touring was and if I'd have trouble finding where to go when I got there, said, "Just go up to the Nordseter and get off the bus. You will immediately see the possibilities."

You couldn't *not* see the possibilities. They're on both sides of the road, undulating off in every direction. Rolling meadows streaked with the breaking-up timberline. Trails wherever you look, some wide enough to accommodate four skiers abreast, others just the two tracks of the solitary trail-maker. You see occasional cabins in the distance, not enough to make you feel the area is cluttered with civilization but enough to feel you most likely would find succor and shelter in an emergency. You have a sense of being alone but not isolated, because from time to time you see an individual or a group skim by.

The main trail goes between Nordseter and Sjusjøen and is marked with red signs on the side toward Nordseter and blue ones on the side toward Sjusjøen. All the little connecting paths have markers of gold. The Lillehammer Tourist Office has available free ski maps showing the complete network of trails between Nordseter, Sjusjøen, Hornsjø, and Pellastova. It's possible, also, to ski from Nordseter back down to your hotel in Lillehammer if you have good snow and one and a half hours of time.

Right next to the bus stop—or as the Norwegians put it, *buss stopp*—there is a place where you can get your *skismørring* (waxing) done for 4 kroner. Lazy waxophile that I am, I did. It was a blue-wax day. I observed carefully and saw the waxer perform what I now think of as the Nordseter variation. He scribbled on a layer of wax and went over it with a torch. He scribbled on another layer and corked it out. Then finally he scribbled on a fairly thick kicker and left it without a touch of either torch or cork. The skis worked perfectly during my whole stay in Lillehammer.

Have your hotel pack you a box lunch to put in your rucksack so you won't have to come home at noon. You'll want to sit under a tree or bask in the sun, resting and enjoying the scene the way the Norwegians do. You can also, with the purchase of a drink, eat your lunch in one of the little eateries by the side of the road. The Hotel Kroner has a nice option. They own a *turisthytta* up on the hill behind the Nevra Hotel. It's a modern cabin with a sundeck overlooking everything, where hotel guests can eat their lunches and buy something to wash them down with.

It's not surprising that this area is the start of Norway's most famous ski marathon, the Birkebeiner. Birkebeiner means "men with birchbark leggings." These were the men who rescued young prince Håkon Håkonsson in 1206. For the 35-mile run of the race the participants have to carry a twelve-pound pack representing the weight of the young prince.

It's not surprising that one might choose to end his ski touring holiday in Lillehammer. Where could you possibly go to top it?

8. SURVIVAL

WHAT'S A chapter on survival doing in a fun book like this? Well, look at it this way. If you go wandering off into the wilderness all ill-prepared and unwary and you freeze to death, it could do a lot toward taking the edge off your good time. And you can die, you know. In ski touring you're not apt to break a bone, but killing yourself is always lurking there as a possibility. Jim Randall, chief ranger of the Rocky Mountain National Park, sums it up, "Mountains don't kill people. People kill themselves in the mountains."

Why does X-C constitute a particular hazard? As Sven Wiik analyzes it, "The big trouble is that because touring is so easy, a lot of people are coming into the sport who aren't really knowledgeable about the outdoors as a whole. And in ski touring there is no one to look out for you."

Just last winter one of these unknowledgeables, a young Coloradan of twenty-one, bought himself a new pair of X-C skis. Since the day was sunny, he was wearing only the proverbial jeans and a light sweater. He set out from his lodge near Boulder. Suddenly the weather turned round. He was not found until the next day. Dead. One mile from the lodge.

It's true that you're not likely to experience a white-out and get lost on your local golf course. And you have almost no chance of destroying yourself on a well-marked trail in, say, Jackson, New Hampshire. Where the trouble comes in is if you park your car in the middle of nowhere and strike out aimlessly. A rain gauge checker who works the San Gabriel Mountains above Los Angeles told me the moment he gets out of sight of his car he figures he has good cause to worry. He's right. He does.

A LITTLE LEARNING IS A SAFE THING: For the skier who wants to do cross-country skiing for the fun of it I cannot recommend too highly the taking of a day-long or overnight survival course. It might very well save your life. Not because such a course will turn you into a winter wilderness wizard able to handle any situation with skill and aplomb. Not at all. It takes years, not hours, to learn how to cope with all the punishment that mother nature can hand out.

The course could save your life, because it will make you realize how incapable you are of taking care of yourself in the wilderness. This should logically lead to a common-sense approach to ski touring. You will never take even one small stupid chance. (One small stupid chance is all you need to take.)

What are the main threats of the winter wilderness? They are frostbite, avalanches, and hypothermia—and the greatest of these is hypothermia.

HYPOTHERMIA: Hypothermia, literally meaning low body temperature, is a new name for an old way to die—exposure. Strangely enough, hypothermia usually occurs when the air temperature is only 40°–50°. This is because when it's colder than that, you realize it's cold and dress accordingly and take sensible precautions.

A typical hypothermic situation takes place in the spring. You're skiing along in light clothing. It's afternoon. You're tired. You're a little soggy from sweat. As the afternoon wanes, the sun's rays thin out. Heading for where you parked the car, you descend into a little valley. The air is colder. A wind comes up. The wind-chill factor, which multiplies the effect of air temperature downward, comes into play. You shiver and wish you'd brought your windbreaker along.

Soon, you're giving off more heat than your body's producing. You shiver uncontrollably now. Your personality changes slightly, but you don't particularly notice this and neither do any of your companions. Anybody can get a little grouchy or dopey at the end of a strenuous day. You become clumsy, maybe stumble. But, again, that's only natural when you're tired. Then you grow a little vague and apathetic. This too may go unnoticed.

Finally you decide you'll just sit down for a while. You

don't want to do anything except just sit. At this point your companions had jolly well better recognize your symptoms and do something for you, because you're totally incapable of doing anything for yourself. You're in a stupor. Your core temperature is falling to 95°–90°–85°. At 78° the heart and lungs stop. You're dead. And the whole process could have taken no more than three hours.

What could your companions have done to save you if they had recognized the symptoms of hypothermia? If they had taken off all their sweaters and jackets and wrapped you in them, it would have shown their concern and good intentions, but it wouldn't have done you one degree of good. Remember, your problem is that your body has stopped producing sufficient heat. They could pile on all the featherbeds that were put on top of the pea for the princess and still you wouldn't have warmed up. What you needed was *external* heat, heat from something or somebody else.

They could have packed a few hot-water bottles around you next to your skin (in the extremely unlikely event that they had a few hot-water bottles handy). Or they could have built a fire, if they had the matches and wood and skill. Lacking those commodities, the only hope left for you was skin to skin contact. This means bare skin, whole body contact with someone whose heat-making mechanism is still working, so that his heat can be transmitted to you. And let's hope you had a sleeping bag to get into or a blanket or tarp to wrap around the two of you, not for modesty's sake, but because it doesn't do too much good to transmit heat to one side of you, if you're giving it off to the cold air on the other.

We can hope that your well-meaning friends didn't give you food, because food diverts blood to your stomach for digestion. Nor should they have given you tea or coffee or that old St. Bernard cure, alcohol. These cause the capillaries to dilate and make you give off the little heat you have left. A small quantity of sugar water is the only approved oral remedy.

It's rather clear from this that the best way to handle hypothermia is not to get it in the first place. You won't, if you remember your five-layer clothing principle. Keep adding and subtracting and don't let yourself get either sweaty or chilled. If you begin shivering, do something about it immediately. And carry a thermometer, if at all possible. You can always diagnose hypothermia by taking a person's temperature. If it's in the low 90s, he's in trouble.

AVALANCHE: Next in our little chronicle of wintertime horrors, we have the avalanche. The U. S. Forest Service puts out a fine brochure entitled "Snow Avalanche; General Rules for Avoiding and Surviving Snow Avalanches." I recommend it, but I don't think it will do all that much good. After all, there are men who have studied avalanches all their lives and have Ph.D.'s in the subject, and they still can't predict with certainty when an avalanche will occur. The only truly effective method of avalanche avoidance and survival is what Mead Hargis, Chief Snow Camping Instructor at Yosemite, calls "the chicken method." The chicken method is simply never ever to go into any area in which there is even the most remote possibility that an avalanche can occur.

If you have any doubts about the advisability of the chicken method, let's have another you-are-there sociodrama.

You are touring with a group, and for some imbecilic reason you decide to cross a slab avalanche danger area. (Slab avalanches are the worst kind. They are usually suddenly triggered by something or somebody and fall in a huge mass, often breaking into large chunks that can be as big as compact pickup trucks.)

One person is elected to cross first. For minimum risk, he picks a high path near the top. The rest of you line up in a straight line, one above the other, and stare hard at the person crossing. If the bad thing happens, this gives you a chance to establish where he was when he was gobbled up by the avalanche and to where he was likely to be carried.

Now, let's say the first person got across. It's your turn next. If you're wearing a pack, you take it off and carry it over one shoulder. You put on your cap, zip up your parka, and take the straps of your poles off your wrists.

You set off following in the tracks of the previous skier. This is not because if one guy made it, the crossing spot is safe. It ain't necessarily so. Ten people could cross and the eleventh could trigger an avalanche. The reason you follow the same path is that you don't want to create any new weaknesses in the snow cover. You don't stop to rest, unless there's some naturally protective feature like a grove of trees or a solid rock you can cower behind. You're moving steadily across. Then it happens. The sharp crack and rumble. Unless you're a superb skier, there's very little chance you can outski it, especially on cross-country skis. (Avalanches have been clocked as fast as 250 miles per hour.) You do what you can about getting rid of everything. You throw off your pack and drop your poles and try to bend over and unhitch your skis. When you're knocked over and tumbled down the hill in a motion like this  over and under the surface of the snow, you try to keep swimming up. Try to do it the most effective way, which is a backstroke with your feet pointed downhill—and lots of luck.

It stops. You try to get your hands in front of your face to scoop the snow away and make a breathing space. But you probably can't, because your arms are pinned down and you're packed in as solidly as if you were frozen in an ice cube. All is dark. Probably there's snow packed around your eyes. You've been rolled around so much you don't know which direction is up. You try to remain calm. (Ha!)

Meanwhile, back on the surface, your companions are looking around desperately for a clue as to where you are —your cap, a glove, a foot, *anything*. They see nothing, so they have to probe. If you're lucky, they've all brought along collapsible ten-foot avalanche probes. If they haven't, they can take the baskets off their ski poles and use them.

They go to the bottom of the avalanche debris and stand about a foot apart. (You may hope you had a lot of companions on this tour.) They stick their poles into the snow in front of them as far as they'll go. If there's no you, they step forward a foot and stick the poles in again. They keep doing this "coarse probe" until they've covered all the territory that they think you might be buried in, based on their careful observance of where you disappeared and the course of the avalanche. If they don't find you in the coarse probe, they go back over the area with a fine probe, shoulder to shoulder, punching the pole in next to each foot as well as in front. You hope they work rapidly, because after one hour you have only a 50 percent chance of surviving.

If you were clever and well prepared, you had a 50-foot avalanche cord tied around your waist. This might have floated to the surface during your tumble down the hill—and might *not* have.

If you were clever and well prepared and well heeled, you were carrying one of those special detection devices that transmits and receives radio signals and costs around $125 a copy. And all of your companions had one too, and it was easy for them to bead in on you.

To keep the story from becoming too grim, let's say you were only six feet under. Most people who are found alive are at that depth or less. And let's say that your fellow tourers managed to find you and dig you out within three hours, the maximum period you can usually survive buried in an avalanche.

They whacked you sharply on the sternum, maybe did a little mouth-to-mouth and got you breathing again. Then they treated you for shock, which anyone of sound mind would have after such an experience.

If the chicken method now has more appeal, other things to beware of besides signs that say "Avalanche Danger, Keep Out" are:

Beware of 30° to 60° slopes. This is where most avalanches occur. Steeper than that the snow has trouble sticking. You can get rock slides from these steeper slopes, and they're fun, too. Shallower than that the likelihood is not too great. Although if conditions are right—that is to say, wrong—almost any slope can avalanche, even one as shallow as 10°.

Beware of storms. Eighty percent of the avalanches occur either during or immediately after a storm.

Beware of the lee side of the mountain. This is the dangerous side. Especially beware of an overhanging cornice, icy pieces of which can fall off and trigger an avalanche, or do their own damage.

Beware of a north-facing slope in winter. The melt and freeze on the south slope stabilizes the snow to a certain extent.

Beware of a south-facing slope in spring. You can get a climax avalanche from the constant melting and refreezing.

Beware of a convex slope. The snow can break apart on the bulge and trigger an avalanche.

Beware of bare or very lightly timbered slopes. Heavy timber and dense underbrush help hold the snow and prevent avalanches.

And finally, when it comes to avalanches, beware even of the things you don't need to beware of.

FROSTBITE: This is the least dangerous of the unholy three. You can't ordinarily be frostbitten to death. If, however, you don't give a case of severe frostbite the proper care, you could conceivably lose as much as a leg.

Frostbite and hypothermia hardly ever go together. Frostbite usually happens in quite cold weather, and although you freeze an extremity, your core body temperature remains normal.

Superficial frostbite, called by some, frostnip, can occur on the cheek, chin, ears, et cetera, as well as the fingers and toes. In the visible areas you can spot it in your companions, first by a redness, then by a grayish-white, waxy appearance. This superficial frostbite can be handled by warming with a warm hand (*not* by rubbing).

Frostbite moves out of the superficial category when the skin loses its resiliency and becomes hard. Then you need attention, preferably medical attention, but at least somebody-who-knows-what-he's-doing attention.

Let's have another traumatic tale. You were skiing along nicely and then you broke a ski tip. You had nothing to repair it with, no spare tip, no tape, no nothing. You had no choice but to walk back. Cross-country boots are fine and warm and comfortable as long as you're skiing in them and generating heat, but walking in them in the snow they give exactly as much protection as tennis shoes. That is to say, none.

Your feet grow numb. They have no feeling. They are frostbitten. Now what do you do? First off, don't stop and try to thaw them out, because if you do, you'll be more than sorry. A thawed-out foot is as painful as a third-degree burn. Walking on it would cause so much damage that it could result in amputation. Better to keep going and try to get to a hospital or somewhere where you can be thawed out and not have to move.

Strangely enough, you can walk for several hours on a frozen foot without doing too much tissue damage. You can't, however, walk even a few yards on a recently thawed one.

The only way to unfreeze an extremity is by the rapid-warming method in which the hand or foot is placed in a container of water heated from 106° to 112°. The hand or foot should not touch the sides or bottom of the container nor should there be a direct source of heat under the container. This is a complex and delicate process and should be done in a hospital, unless there is absolutely no way to get to one.

Most of the damage in frostbite is caused by the sharp ice crystals cutting up the cells as the thawing takes place. The good old-fashioned frostbite treatment of rubbing briskly is the worst thing you can do. Using this method you can, just like magic, turn a frostbitten toe into an amputated foot.

All in all, rather than to go through all this freeze and thaw, it's better to protect your frostbite-vulnerable extremities with warm coverings. Never handle cold metal objects with your bare hands. If the work is too delicate to do in regular mittens or gloves, use a pair of silk gloves. And, finally, always carry a spare ski tip, if you're going off the beaten track or tamped-down road. As Hildegard Knef said in *The Gift Horse*, "How far everything is when one has to walk."

Your aching pack: After one X-C evening in Steamboat Springs, Sven Wiik unloaded his backpack for a group of us, so we could see what he carried. Out came:

an extra wool sweater

a collapsible triangular saw

a collapsible shovel

a drinking cup

a storm kit composed of matches and a candle for fire-starting, salt to counteract fatigue, a whistle for signaling, sugar cubes, bouillon cubes, tea bags, wire, sealing tape, an 80″ x 96″ plastic tube in bright yellow suitable for shelter and signaling, and a brochure on signaling. (The lid of the kit could also be used for signaling and the kit itself as a cooking pot.)

a whole gang of tools and parts that could fix anything that might happen to skis, poles, or bindings and fix it in *five minutes.*

a spare ski tip that converts to a saw when you open it up and could also be used to scoop out snow for a shelter.

a spare pole basket, a pole point, and a grip for a ski pole

a multipurpose knife

tape

extra waxes

a first-aid kit

a lip chap stick

two oranges and an apple (These were leftovers; he always took more, and more basic foods than this.)

And there may have been a few things I missed, since my eyes were spinning as everything possible seemed to emerge except a partridge in a pear tree. It appeared to my un-wilderness-oriented eyes that Sven had enough in that pack to spend three months in Siberia.

Naïvely I asked, "But you wouldn't take all that on just a day-tour, would you?"

Sven, who is normally the most amiable and soft-spoken of men, clouded over like a storm out of the north. "I would take all that on just a *half*-day tour," he boomed off the rafters.

He would. And so, I later learned, would anyone who knew what he was doing. If you're going out touring and you're not on marked, well-traveled trails, you have to assume that you may have to spend the night out in the snow. You pack your pack accordingly.

Since it is a literal drag to have to tote a packful of emergency gear every time you want to get away from it all or them all, we can all hope for and, more important, work for, the day when there are many marked trails and scattered along them at appropriate intervals well-stocked survival cabins. To see a perfect model of what can be done, hie yourself to Quebec, Canada. There, in three parks, each within a half-hour drive of the center of town, you'll find a total of 140 miles of cross-country trails. All are clearly marked and mapped and accurately graded according to difficulty and beautifully maintained by the government. There are oil-stove-heated warming huts and restrooms at strategic locations. These parks are fantastically good and fantastically safe places to ski. If Canada can do it, why can't we? All it takes is enthusiasm for the project and organization to carry it out.

Although X-C is a sport for people who basically dislike and distrust organized activities, this kind of organization will be beneficial to us all. And the life you save may be you-know-whose.

Skill on the hill: Having the wherewithal to spend the night isn't enough, though. You have to know how to use what's in your pack. It's the same principle as taking along a spare and a jack when you travel a deserted road and having no idea how to change a tire. A shovel won't dig a snow cave to shelter you without your cooperation and direction. A fire won't spontaneously combust for your warmth and comfort.

Therefore, if you ever intend to take the chances that may get you into a situation in which you'll be forced to care for yourself and perhaps care for others overnight, you need to practice your survival skills. Even if you take a survival course—one with overnight sleeping in a snow cave—you'll still need to do the whole act several times on your own.

The main reason for this is to prevent panic under pressure. The only time you'd ever be doing this survival bit would be when something untoward happened, such as the weather suddenly becoming stormy or a member of your party getting sick or injured or finding that you were lost and night was coming on. Such untoward situations as these can easily induce a chicken-with-its-head-cut-off panic in those who aren't totally confident that they have the ability to handle the situation. And panic can be as dangerous to your winter survival as an avalanche. I think what can happen in panic is summed up beautifully in the Mountain Rescue Association's brochure on fatigue and exhaustion: "In panic a man can run two hours, walk two hours, crawl an hour, then lie down from exhaustion for eternity."

DIGGING IT: Yosemite's Mead Hargis suggests that you drive your car up into some safe place in snow country, park it, dig yourself a snow cave right next to the car, and sleep in it (the cave, not the car). In case you flunk the test, your car is there ready to haul you off.

To dig a snow cave you need a drift about four or five feet deep. It needs to be this deep so you can make the roof and walls and floor around seven inches thick. Often you can find drifts around logs or rocks and they can help create one of your walls. Then you just dig your heart and liver and pancreas and all your other innards out.

You're supposed to keep the entrance small in order not to let in the snow and wind. That's another of those supposed-tos that aren't particularly easy to carry off. It's a heckuva job to lie in that little entrance and dig a huge hollow inside and it's an even worse job to haul the snow out a small opening. But that's snow cave biz.

Let's assume you've hollowed out your interior, and it's

large enough for you to get into and turn around in without brushing against the walls and getting wet. Then for insulation it's a good idea to spread a ground cloth, if you have one. If you don't, boughs will do the same job, if you can find them.

If you're a real snow cave freak (not likely, if you've read this far in this book), you can make your frosty pad more comfortable by cutting out bunks and shelves along the wall and glazing the walls and ceiling by going over them with a lighted candle.

On the other hand, if the whole idea of snow cave digging bores and distresses you, then perhaps you're more the snow trench type. It's a much faster procedure and can be done anywhere and in any kind of snow. It only takes a half hour to forty-five minutes to dig a trench.

All you do is dig out a coffin-size-and-shape hole in the snow. (Sorry about that comparison, but it's the most accurate description there is.) Line the bottom with a ground cloth or boughs and make a cover out of branches and a tarp or more boughs.

None of these shelters is exactly the Savoy for overnight comfort, but you can say one thing for them. They beat dying all hollow.

READ THEM SO YOU WON'T HAVE TO WEEP: The Mountain Rescue Council, Tacoma Unit (P.O. Box 696, Tacoma, Washington, 98401) can be your first line of defense in survival situations. They publish an outstanding series of safety brochures: "Survival," "Fatigue-Exhaustion-Energy," "Street Signs of the Wilderness" (Compass Orienteering), and "Hiking and Backpacking Safety." These are all free for the ordering, but you should at least donate the postage for their just cause of "saving lives through rescue and safety education." Also, you should buy one of everything they have for sale: the storm kit ($2) and the books on *Outdoor Living* ($2.50) and *Mountaineering Medicine* ($1) and "A Survival Lecture Outline" (50¢).

THE HANDWRITING ON THE WALL: This particular handwriting is on the wall of a hotel in Norway and it makes a lot more sense than *mene, mene, tekel, upharsin,* when it comes to keeping ski tourers from their own destruction:

Never go alone.

Leave a message giving your route before starting.

Show respect for the weather and for the forecast.

Take a map, compass, sufficient clothing, a rucksack, and food.

Return in time, there is no disgrace in turning back.

Save energy by seeking shelter in time—dig a snow cave if necessary.

Norwegians, incidentally, have little patience for those who commit a dumbness on a ski tour. You're billed for the cost of your rescue—and that can add up to a bundle of kroner.

KNOW THY ENEMY: That takes care of nature. There is also something very unnatural, in fact, contrary to nature, that we have to fear. Roaring monsters threaten us at every turn in the trail. In case you don't recognize what

I'm talking about, it's those wintertime obscenities, polluter scooters, or, as they prefer to be called, snowmobiles.

Not only do they threaten us, they totally ruin our trails by heating up the snow so that it melts and refreezes into a solid sheet. When the next motorized marauder comes along, he breaks up the surface into chunks. Just try to ski on that.

I don't advocate physical violence toward snowmobilers, although they certainly deserve it. I do, however, advocate scowling and tooth-baring and fist-shaking and appropriate expletive hurling. I also advocate working toward the beautiful law that they have in Switzerland. No snowmobiles are allowed except to do necessary work, such as trail-cutting and emergency rescue operations—and even that is closely watched. The Far Hills Inn brightens their brochure and the ski touring days of those who go there with the stern admonition, "For the safety of guests—SNOWMOBILES NOT PERMITTED."

SHAPING UP WITH X-C: One final safety admonition concerns your own physical condition. Naturally you wouldn't sign on for a rugged all-day tour if you were in lousy shape, if for no other reason than that you'd ruin the excursion for everyone else—a tour has to march to the drumbeat of its weakest skier.

To find out what kind of shape you're in, you might try Kenneth Cooper's *Aerobics* 12-minute test. See how much ground you can cover in this amount of time. You can run, jog, walk, or do any combination thereof. Your rating is as follows:

THE 12-MINUTE TEST

DISTANCE COVERED IN 12 MINUTES (MILES)		YOUR PHYSICAL CONDITION IS:
MEN	WOMEN	
1.00 or less	.94 or less	Lousy
1.00 to 1.24	.95 to 1.14	Poor
1.25 to 1.49	1.15 to 1.34	Fair
1.50 to 1.75	1.35 to 1.64	Good
1.75 or more	1.65 or more	Excellent

Note: You shouldn't even do the test without your doctor's permission, if you have some serious medical problem or if you are in the untrustworthy over-thirty bracket.

If you turn out to be in lousy or poor shape, go for two-hour tours until you build yourself up a little. Fair to good, make it a half day at first. If you're in excellent shape, keep going as long as you feel like it. You probably will, anyway, since you're no doubt some kind of physical fanatic.

Aside from pacing yourself until you shape up with X-C, if you're practicing the sport strictly for the fun of it, all you really need to do is follow the advice of that ninety-seven-year-old X-C wonderman, Jack Rabbit Johannsen:

Daily exercise is important. Even city people can manage it by walking to their offices, their schools, or stores. Never ride if it is possible to walk. Don't use elevators. Eat only if hungry. Never from habit. If you look after your body, your body will look after you.

THE LAST WORD

Finally as you embark upon your ski touring trail through life, I'd like to leave you with some sage counsel by the immortal philosopher Satchel Paige:

Keep the juices flowing by jangling gently as you move.

Go very lightly on the vices, such as carrying on in society. The social ramble ain't restful.

Don't look back. Something may be gaining on you.

God Tur!

APPENDICES

APPENDIX A

Classification of Cross-Country Skiers

BEGINNER: A skier who has never been on a trail before. He should only be taken on gentle fields or meadows over short distances.

NOVICE: A skier who can ski under good control with a good snowplow turn and be able to safely descend a trail up to 15 degrees.

INTERMEDIATE: A skier, experienced, who can negotiate most all trails and has good control on descents up to 30 degrees.

ADVANCED/EXPERT: A very hardy type who can take any trail at reasonable speed and bushwhack through rough country.

Courtesy of Far West Ski Association

APPENDIX B

Great World Waxing Guide

The proper wax for touring and cross-country skiing depends on the type of snow, how long it has settled on the ground, and the moisture content. By selecting a number from each of the questions opposite, in sequence, you can identify a snow type. Waxes for the snow type are then listed in the table by manufacturer; only numbers corresponding to real snow types appear. →

	Manufacturer's Brand Name:				
Snow Type:	RODE	EX-ELIT	SWIX	REX	BRATLIE
111	Dk Gn	Lt Gn	Lt Gn	Turquoise	Brown (Silke)
112	Lt Gn	Green	Green	Lt Gn/Gn	Brown
113	Blue	Blue	Blue	Blue	Brown
114	Violet	Violet	Violet	Violet	Blue (Blanding)
115	Yellow	Tö Klis	Red Klis	Yellow	Black (Klistervoks)
116	Red Klis Yel Klis	Tö Med Tjara K	Yel Klis	Red Klis	Black Klister
123	Lt Gn	Green	Green	Green	Brown
124	Blue	Blue	Blue	Blue	Blue and Green Klister
125	Violet	Violet	Violet	Violet	Black Klister
126	Red	Red	Red	Red	Black Klister
127	Red Klis	Tö Med Tjara K	Red Klis	Red Klis	Black Klister
226	Vio Klis	Tö Klis	Vio Klis	Vio Klis	Red Klister
227	Vio Klis Silv Kl	Tö Med Tjara K	Red Klis	Silver Klis	Black Klister
228	Blue Klis	Skare K	Blue Klis	Blue Klis	Red

N.B. Type 124 is the most common!

SNOW TYPE:

Is the surface . . .

1. Snow? **2.** Ice, crust, corn, or pellets?

Is it snowing or has it snowed in the last few days?

1. Yes! **2.** No!

A handful of snow . . .

1. is very powdery.
2. blows easily.
3. blows with difficulty.
4. forms a loose clump.
5. balls up easily.
6. drips water when squeezed.
7. is a mixture of snow and water.
8. too icy; cannot be had.

EXAMPLE:

→ **112** See chart for best wax to choose.

Manufacturer's Brand Name:

TOKO	HOLMENKOL	VAUHTI	ØSTBYE
Green	Green	Blue No. 3	Special
Green	Green	Green No. 2	Mix
Blue	Blue	Orange No. 1	Mix, Medium
Violet	Violet, Red	Red No. 4	Medium, Klistervox
Yellow	Violet	Red Klister No. 5	Klistervox
Red Klister	Yellow Klister	Red Klister No. 5	Klister
Green	Green	Green No. 2	Special, Mix
Blue	Blue	Orange No. 1	Mix
Violet	Violet	Red No. 4	Mixolin, Klistervox
Red	Yellow Klister	Red Klister No. 5	Mixolin
Red Klister	Yellow Klister	Red Klister No. 5	Klister
Violet Klister	Red Klister	Mixed No. 1 and 4 Klister	Mixolinvox, Mixolin
Red Klister	Silver Klister	Red Klister No. 5	Klister
Blue Klister	Blue Klister	Blue Klister No. 6	Skare

Courtesy of Great World, Inc., West Simsbury, Conn. 06092.

APPENDIX C

Mountaincraft Waxing Guide for Rocky Mountain Conditions

	Snow type and characteristics	Temperature Range C°	Temperature Range F°	Wax and Brand
Falling and New Snow	Extremely Dry (new powder)	-8 ↓	18 ↓	Bratlie Brown (thin)
	Very Dry (blows easily)	-5 ↓	21 ↓	Bratlie Brown (heavier kicker)
	Dry (blows with difficulty)	0 to 5	23 to32	Swix Blue
	Transition (clumps in hand)	-1 to +1	30 to 34	Swix Violet
	Mushy (rolling snowballs dig in)	0 to +3	32 to 37	Bratlie Klistervoks ●
	Wet (hand soaking wet when squeezing)	+2 to +6	35 to 42	Rex Red Klister ●
Settled Snow	Very Dry (small crystals blow)	-12 ↓	10 ↓	Bratlie Brown
	Dry (small crystals will form snowballs)	-1 to -10	14 to 30	Swix Blue
	Transition (lg. crystals, corn)	-1 to +1	30 to 34	Bratlie Black Klister
	Mushy (hand wet after squeezing)	0 to +3	32 to 37	Bratlie Black Klister
	Wet (slushy)	+2 to +6	35 to 42	Bratlie Black Klister
●●	Dry, Hard Crust Ice, etc.	-5 ↓	21 ↓	Rex Blue Klister ●
	Crusty, but softer to Mushy and Wet	-6 to +1	22 to 34	Rex Violet Klister
	Wet Slush	0 to +6	32 to 42	Bratlie Black Klister

●● Metamorphosed snow
(Old snow which melts, freezes, etc.)

● Not included since these conditions are not commonly encountered.

General Instructions:

Begin with a thin layer of wax for the coldest conditions to be encountered, add a thicker kicker if additional bite is needed. If that isn't sufficient, use the next warmer range wax, first as a kicker, then full length.

Courtesy of Mountaincraft, Steamboat Springs, Colo.

APPENDIX D

Boot Size Conversions

Women's Boots

U.S.	5	5½	6	6½	7	7½	8	8½	9	9½
European	35	36	37	37	38	38½	39	40	41	

Men's Boots

U.S.	7	7½	8	8½	9	9½	10	10½	11
European	39	40	41	42	43	43	44	44	45
U.S.	11½	12	12½						
European	45	46	46						

APPENDIX E

Mail Order Sources for Equipment and Clothing

AKERS SKI
Andover, Maine 042216
skis, boots, bindings, poles, waxes, torches, ski bags, snow thermometers, Swedish touring suits, Swedish warmup suits, gloves and mitten, hats, socks, gaiters, night head lights

EDDIE BAUER
P.O. Box 3700
Seattle, Washington 98124
rucksacks, parkas, knickers, gloves and mittens, socks, underwear, turtlenecks, sweaters

L. L. BEAN, INC.
Freeport, Maryland 04032
skis, boots, bindings, poles, waxes, rucksacks, parkas, knickers, gloves and mittens, turtlenecks, hats, sweaters, socks, underwear

EASTERN MOUNTAIN SPORTS, INC.
1041 Commonwealth Ave.
Boston, Mass. 02215
skis, boots, bindings, poles, waxes, torches, knickers, touring suits, gloves and mittens, turtlenecks, hats, sweaters, socks, underwear, gaiters

GREAT WORLD, INC.
250 Farms Village Road
P.O. Box 250
West Simsbury, Connecticut 06092
skis, boots, bindings, poles, waxes, torches, compasses, gloves, hats, sweaters, socks, underwear, spats and gaiters

HUSFLIDEN
Postboks 19
Trondheim, Norway
handknit Norwegian wool sweaters and hats

KELTY
1801 Victory Blvd.
Glendale, California 91201
skis, boots, bindings, poles, waxes, torches, parkas, mittens, hats, socks, underwear, gaiters

KLOVER HUSET
Strandgaten 13
5001 Bergen, Norway
handknit Norwegian wool sweaters and hats

PAUL MAGE I/S
22 Oestergade
DK-110
Copenhagen, Denmark
handknit Danish wool sweaters

MOOR & MOUNTAIN
Concord, Massachusetts 01742
skis, boots, bindings, poles, waxes, torches, parkas, ski touring suits, gloves and mittens, hats, sweaters, socks, underwear, gaiters

CARROLL REED
North Conway, New Hampshire 03860
Trak skis, bindings, boots, poles, parkas, knickers, hats, turtlenecks, sweaters, underwear

SKI HUT
1615 University Avenue
Berkeley, California 94703
skis, boots, bindings, poles, compasses, thermometers, parkas, knickers, gloves and mittens, sweaters, socks, underwear, rucksacks

TIMBERLINE HOUSE LTD.
3394 South Broadway
Englewood, Colorado 80110
skis, boots, bindings, poles, waxes, parkas, knickers, gloves and mittens, sweaters, underwear, gaiters, rucksacks

X-C-S
The X-Country Shop
P.O. Box 447
Republic, Michigan 49879
skis, boots, bindings, poles, waxes, torches, rucksacks

APPENDIX F

Special Cross-Country Touring and Teaching Programs

AMC CROSS-COUNTRY SKI PROGRAM
AMC Northern New England Regional Office
Pinkham Notch Camp
Gorham, New Hampshire 03581

COPPER CROSS-COUNTRY
P.O. Box 397
Frisco, Colorado 80443

ROYAL GORGE SKI TOURING SCHOOL
% The Ski Hut
1615 University Ave.
Berkeley, California 94703

SILENT TOURS
% Mountaincraft Shop
810 Lincoln Ave.
Steamboat Springs, Colorado 80477

SUGAR HOUSE
P.O. Box 5436
South Lake Tahoe, California 95795

WILDERNESS ALLIANCE
Route 2, Box 12D
Conifer, Colorado 80433

WILDERNESS EXPERIENCE
P.O. Box 1042
Canoga Park, California 91304

APPENDIX G

Ski Touring Organizations

(Write for membership information, benefits, etc.)

SKI TOURING ASSOCIATION
Box Nine
West Simsbury, Conn. 06092

SKI TOURING COUNCIL
R. F. Mattesich, Pres.
Troy, Vt. 05868

APPENDIX H

Resorts with Cross-Country Facilities and Programs

ALASKA

Alyeska

Accommodations: Nugget Inn
Equipment Rental: Alyeska Resort
Instruction: no
Trails: 2½, 3, 5, and 10-kilometer trails
Address: Alyeska Resort, Inc.
Girdwood, Alaska 990587

Fairbanks

Accommodations: town
Equipment Rental: Clem's Upholstery in town and Nordic Ski Cellar at the University of Alaska
Instruction: individual instructors; University of Alaska Short Courses
Trails: a vast complex of 2½, 4, 6, and 12-mile trails around the University of Alaska; some are competitive only
Address: Nordic Ski Club of Fairbanks
Box 80111
College, Alaska 99701

CALIFORNIA

Bear Valley

Accommodations: all resort lodges
Equipment Rental: Bear Valley Sport Shop
Instruction: Mt. Reba Ski School
Trails: not specified in brochure; half-day and overnight guided tours

Address: Bear Valley Sport Shop
P.O. Box 5
Bear Valley, Calif. 95223

Hope Valley

Accommodations: Sorenson's Resort; South Lake Tahoe lodges are 20 miles away

Equipment Rental: Viggo Ski Shop

Instruction: Viggo Nordic Ski School

Trails: not specified in brochure; half-day, full-day, and overnight guided tours

Address: Viggo Nordic Ski School
Sorenson's Resort
Hope Valley, Calif. 96139

Kirkwood

Accommodations: lodges at South Lake Tahoe

Equipment Rental: Kirkwood Touring Center

Instruction: Kirkwood Touring Center

Trails: not specified in brochure; half-day, full-day, and overnight guided tours

Address: Kirkwood Touring Center
Kirkwood, Calif. 95696

Lassen Park

Accommodations: Pine Cottages or Drakesbad Guest Ranch in the park; Childs Meadows Resort, Deer Creek Lodge, Fire Mountain Lodge, Mill Creek Resort, Minera Lodge outside the park

Equipment Rental: Childs Meadows Resort

Instruction: Childs Meadows Resort

Trails: marked 2½-mile course; trails from a few miles in length to a 27-mile loop through the park

Address: Childs Meadows Resort
Highway 36E
Mill Creek, Calif. 96061

Mammoth

Accommodations: all resort lodges; Tamarack Lodge is headquarters for X-C

Equipment Rental: Tamarack Lodge

Instruction: Cal-Nordic Ski Touring Institute

Trails: some marked trails; half-day, full-day, and overnight guided tours

Address: Cal-Nordic Ski Touring Institute
Tamarack Lodge
Mammoth Lakes, Calif. 93546

Olympic Valley

Accommodations: Big Chief Resort

Equipment Rental: Big Chief Cross-Country Ski School

Instruction: Big Chief Cross-Country Ski School

Trails: not specified in brochure; full-day and overnight guided tours

Address: Big Chief Cross-Country Skiing
P.O. Box 2477
Olympic Valley, Calif. 95730

Yosemite

Accommodations: Camp Curry, Yosemite Lodge, Ahwahnee Hotel

Equipment Rental: Mountain Shop in the village

Instruction: Yosemite Mountaineering

Trails: prepared tracks and numerous trails; day and overnight guided tours

Address: Yosemite Mountaineering
Yosemite Park and Curry Co.
Yosemite National Park, Calif. 95389

COLORADO

Aspen

Accommodations: all resort lodges

Equipment Rental: Ashcroft Ski Tours Unlimited; Chuck Fothergill's Outdoor Sportsman

Instruction: Ashcroft Ski Tours Unlimited; Chuck Fothergill's Outdoor Sportsman

Trails: 20 miles of groomed trails; day and overnight tours

Address: Ashcroft Ski Tours Unlimited
Box 1572
Aspen, Colo. 81611

or

Chuck Fothergill's Outdoor Sportsman
Box 88
Aspen, Colo. 81611

Steamboat Springs

Accommodations: Scandinavian Lodge
Equipment Rental: Scandinavian Lodge
Instruction: Sven Wiik Ski School
Trails: 4 prepared tracks; half-day and full-day guided tours
Address: Scandinavian Lodge
Box 129
Steamboat Springs, Colo. 80477

Vail

Accommodations: all resort lodges
Equipment Rental: Steve Rieschl's Touring School
Instruction: Steve Rieschl's Touring School
Trails: a network of 20 trails; 125 miles in all
Address: Vail Resort Association
Vail, Colo. 81657

MAINE

Sugarloaf

Accommodations: all resort lodges
Equipment Rental: Harvey Boynton Ski Shop; Ski Rack Shop
Instruction: Sugarloaf Ski School
Trails: 4, 7, and 9-mile trails
Address: Sugarloaf Area Association
Kingfield, Me. 04947

MICHIGAN

Boyne

Accommodations: all resort lodges
Equipment Rental: Othmar Schneider Ski School
Instruction: Othmar Schneider Ski School
Trails: 10, 15, 20, and 30-kilometer courses; guided all-day tours

Address: Othmar Schneider Ski School
Nordic Division
Boyne Country
Boyne Mountain Lodge
Boyne Falls, Mich. 49713

NEW HAMPSHIRE

Grantham

Accommodations: Gray Ledges
Instruction: Gray Ledges
Trails: extensive network over fields and through woods
Address: Gray Ledges
Grantham, N. H. 03753

Jackson

Accommodations: all resort lodges
Equipment Rental: at many lodges and at Jackson Ski Touring Center
Instruction: Jack Frost Ski School; Black Mt. Ski School
Trails: 70-mile network; overnight guided tours from Pinkham Notch
Address: Jackson Ski Touring Center
Jackson, N. H. 03846

NEW YORK

Lake Placid

Accommodations: Adirondak Loj
Equipment Rental: Adirondak Loj
Instruction: Ursula Schniebs Ski Touring School
Trails: extensive network; connection to 12-mile trail complex of Mt. Van Hoevenberg Recreation Area; also touring on Lake Placid Lake
Address: Adirondak Loj
Box 867
Lake Placid, N. Y. 12946

UTAH

Park City

Accommodations: all resort lodges
Equipment Rental: Wolfe's, Timberhaus, Miner's Find
Instruction: Park City Resort Ski School
Trails: 8-kilometer course through golf course; old mine trails; guided day tours
Address: Park City Resort Reservation Center
Box 919
Park City, Utah 84060

VERMONT

Chittenden

Accommodations: Mountain Top Inn
Equipment Rental: Mountain Top Inn
Instruction: Mountain Top Ski School
Trails: a prepared network
Address: Mountain Top Inn
Chittenden, Vt. 05737

East Burke

Accommodations: Darion Inn
Equipment Rental: Darion Inn X-C Shop; Burke Mountain Ski Shop
Instruction: Burke Mountain Ski School
Trails: 22 miles marked trails; guided tours; overnight excursions at McGill Touring Camp
Address: Darion Inn
East Burke, Vt. 05832
or
Burke Mountain Recreation
East Burke, Vt. 05832

Goshen

Accommodations: Blueberry Hill Farm
Equipment Rental: Blacksmith Shop at the Farm
Instruction: no
Trails: 30 miles of trails

Address: Blueberry Hill Farm
Brandon, Vt. 05733

Stowe

Accommodations: Trapp Family Lodge
Equipment Rental: Trapp Family Lodge
Instruction: Trapp Family Lodge
Trails: over 50 miles of marked trails; guided day tours
Address: Trapp Family Lodge
Stowe, Vt. 05672

Sugarbush

Accommodations: Sugarbush Inn
Equipment Rental: Sugarbush Inn
Instruction: Sugarbush Inn
Trails: 30 miles of marked trails; all-day and overnight guided trips
Address: Sugarbush Inn
Warren, Vt. 05674

Woodstock

Accommodations: Woodstock Inn
Equipment Rental: Woodstock Ski Touring Center
Instruction: Woodstock Ski Touring Center
Trails: tracks on the golf course and several trails
Address: The Woodstock Inn
Woodstock, Vt. 05091

WYOMING

Jackson Hole

Accommodations: hotels in Jackson Hole and all lodges at Teton Village
Equipment Rental: Rick Horn Wilderness Expeditions; Jack Pine Ski Rental Shop; Jackson Hole Ski and Sports
Instruction: Rick Horn Wilderness Expeditions; Jack Pine Ski Rental Shop; Powderhorn Ski Tours; Sundance Ski Tours
Trails: extensive network through Grand Teton National Park and Yellowstone National Park; day and overnight tours

Address: Rick Horn
Wilderness Expeditions
Box 471
Jackson, Wyo. 83001
or
Quiet Country Ski Tours
Jack Pine Ski Rental Shop
P.O. Box 1904
Jackson, Wyo. 83001
or
Sundance Ski Tours, Box 1226, Jackson, Wyo. 83001

QUEBEC, CANADA

Mont-Tremblant

Accommodations: various lodges at and near Mont-Tremblant
Equipment Rental: some lodges
Instruction: some monitors available
Trails: 82 miles marked trails; 5 for beginners, 4 for intermediates, 2 for experts; network is in Mont-Tremblant Park and is maintained by the government
Address: Parks Branch
5075 Fullum Street
Montreal, Canada
and
Laurentian Resorts Association
1500 Stanely, Room 411
Montreal, Canada

Quebec

Accommodations: hotels in Quebec
Equipment Rental: Reception Center at Laurentides Park; Alpine shop at Mont-Sainte-Anne
Instruction: some monitors available
Trails: Laurentides Park—22 miles marked trails; 6 for begin-

ners, 4 for intermediates, 3 for experts; 3 warming cabins
Mont-Sainte-Anne Park—81 miles marked trails; 3, 12, 18, and 30 mile runs; 2 warming cabins; guided tours

Address: Marc Hardy, Director
Tourist Information Division
Department of Tourism, Fish & Game Complex G,
620 Cyrille Blvd. East Quebec, Canada
and
Hospitality, Hotels and Tours
P.O. Box 9
Haute-Ville
Quebec, Canada

Val Morin

Accommodations: Far Hills Inn
Equipment Rental: Far Hills Inn
Instruction: Far Hills Inn Ski School
Trails: 50 miles marked and groomed; half-day guided tours
Address: Far Hills Inn
Val Morin, Quebec,
Canada

APPENDIX I

Alpine Resorts with Ski Touring Facilities

AUSTRIA

Badgastein, Heiligenblut, Igls, Kirchberg, Kitzbühel, Lech, Obertauern, Radstadt in Tirol, St. Johann, Schruns, Seefeld

FRANCE

L'Alpe d'Huez, Autrans, Ax-les-Thermes, Bessans, La Bresse, Chamonix, Châtel, La Clusaz, Combloux, Les Contamines, Courchevel, Gérardmer, Megève, Morzine, Saint-Gervais, Saint-Pierre-de-Chartreuse, Samoëns, Le Sauze, Vars, Villard-de-lans

GERMANY

Berchtesgaden, Garmisch

ITALY

Cortina d'Ampezzo, Corvara in Badia, Madonna di Campiglio, Ponte di Legno, Selva (Val Gardena), Tonale

SWITZERLAND

Adelboden, Amden, Arosa, Braunwald, Crans-sur-Sierre, Davos, Engelberg, Flims, Grindelwald, Gstaad, Kandersteg, Klosters, Malbrun, Montana, Pontresina, St. Moritz, Villars, Wildhaus, Zuoz

APPENDIX J

Cross-Country Races to Enter for the Fun of It

(Write for dates, routes, entry information, etc.)

Canadian Marathon Ski Tour
The Viking Ski Club, P.O. Box 57
Morin Heights, Que., Canada
Frisco Gold Rush
P.O. Box X-L
Frisco, Colo. 80443
Glacier Stampede
Alaska Alpine Club
Box 81200
College, Alaska 99701
Great Race
Ski Touring Association
Box 208
West Simsbury, Conn. 06092
John Craig Memorial Cross Country Ski Race and Mail Run
Ann Bjorn
12925 S.W. Faircrest
Portland, Ore. 97225
Keystone Cross Country Caper
Keystone International
Bob Kluge
Box 38
Dillon, Colo. 80435
Nordic Holiday Weekend
Yosemite Montaineering
Yosemite Park and Curry Co.
Yosemite National Park, Calif. 95389
Stowe Derby
Box 281
Stowe, Vt. 05672
Washington's Birthday Cross-Country Ski Touring Race
R.D. 2, Box 185
Brattleboro, Vt. 05301

APPENDIX K

Distance Medal Events Program Fact Sheet

Requirements for medals

The mileage required for each medal is:

Bronze	75
Silver	150
Gold	300

Only one medal is awarded against each log. If the participant retains the log to ski additional mileage for a higher award, only the highest medal will be awarded. A participant can send in the log for the lower award and then start again with a new log to try and achieve one of the higher awards.

The mileage is logged after each day's skiing by the participant. Any terrain or location may be used in attaining these medals. On measured terrain use the linear map distance plus 10 percent for terrain adjustment. Help in completing the log is available at place of purchase or any outlet where the Distance Medal Events placard is displayed.

Membership is not required to participate in Distance Medal Events but when the mileage has been achieved membership in the United States Ski Association is required for the award of the medal, or the subscription price of $7.00 must be mailed with the log.

When completed the log should be mailed to:

Distance Medal Events
United States Ski Association
1726 Champa, Suite 300
Denver, Colo. 80202

The President's Council on Physical Fitness and Sports

This program is being administered in cooperation with The President's Council on Physical Fitness and Sports.

Logs and rules for the President's Council award may be obtained from the USSA national office or:

The President's Council on Physical Fitness & Sports
Washington, D.C. 20202

11/1/72

APPENDIX L

Wind Chill Factor Table

When the temperature/wind speed factor falls in the area shaded below, frostbite, especially of the face, is a serious hazard. Don't forget that speed of skiing or snowmobiling counts as "wind speed" in figuring chill factor.

When Thermometer Reads	When the wind blows at the m.p.h. below, it reduces Temperature to								
	Calm	5	10	15	20	25	30	35	40
+50	50	48	40	36	32	30	28	27	26
+40	40	37	28	22	18	16	13	11	10
+30	30	27	16	9	4	0	−2	−4	−6
+20	20	16	4	−5	−10	−15	−18	−20	−21
+10	10	6	−9	−18	−25	−29	−33	−35	−37
0	0	−5	−21	−36	−39	−44	−48	−49	−53
−10	−10	−15	−33	−45	−53	−59	−63	−67	−69
−20	−20	−26	−46	−58	−67	−74	−79	−82	−85
−30	−30	−36	−58	−72	−82	−88	−94	−98	−100
−40	−40	−47	−70	−88	−96	−104	−109	−113	−116
−50	−50	−57	−85	−99	−110	−118	−125	−129	−132
−60	−60	−68	−95	−112	−124	−133	−140	−145	−148

To measure speed of wind without instruments: When CALM (smoke rises vertically); 1-12 m.p.h. (just feel wind on face, leaves in motion); 13-24 (raises dust or loose paper, snow drifts, branches move); 25-30 (large branches move, wires whistle); 30-40 (whole trees in motion, hard to walk against).

For the properly clothed, there is little danger down to -20° but caution should be used with regard to all exposed flesh. At below -20°, take no unnecessary chances.

Courtesy of Great World, West Simsbury, Conn.